The Struggle to Define God

The Struggle to Define God

Dissent in Postexilic Judah

ROBERT A. BUTTERFIELD

WIPF & STOCK · Eugene, Oregon

THE STRUGGLE TO DEFINE GOD
Dissent in Postexilic Judah

Copyright © 2017 Robert A. Butterfield. All rights reserved. Except for brief quotations in critical publications or reviews, no part of this book may be reproduced in any manner without prior written permission from the publisher. Write: Permissions, Wipf and Stock Publishers, 199 W. 8th Ave., Suite 3, Eugene, OR 97401.

Wipf & Stock
An Imprint of Wipf and Stock Publishers
199 W. 8th Ave., Suite 3
Eugene, OR 97401

www.wipfandstock.com

PAPERBACK ISBN: 978-1-5326-1789-8
HARDCOVER ISBN: 978-1-4982-4296-7
EBOOK ISBN: 978-1-4982-4295-0

Manufactured in the U.S.A.   APRIL 5, 2017

Contents

Acknowledgments | vii
A Note on Method | ix
Introduction | xi

Ruth | 1
Jonah | 17
Job | 29
Rahab | 55

Final reflections | 61
Bibliography | 77

Acknowledgments

I wish to thank my brother, Dr. Bruce A. Butterfield, whose editorial assistance has been invaluable to me. My thanks also go out to the Rev. Dr. Jerry L. Folk and the Rev. Dr. Frederick Trost for their helpful comments on the final chapter. Any errors in this book are, of course, entirely my own.

A Note on Method

HUNDREDS OF SCHOLARLY OPINIONS have been published on the books of Jonah, Job, and Ruth and on the story of Rahab. These opinions all have a certain authority, but to fully respect a literary text is to allow it to speak for itself. This book presupposes that a literary text is perfectly capable of speaking for itself, in the sense that every text is or creates its own logical universe. Analyzing every element of that universe and showing how its elements function in relation to each other should clarify what the text is trying to do. In short, the text is its own authority and does not require confirmation from outside the text. Seen in this perspective, the task of the reader or critic is to understand the universe of the text and follow its logic to the conclusions to which the text itself points.

Since the aim of this book is to learn from these four biblical texts and to apply that learning to the wider world, it will be necessary to reflect on the impact that these texts had on postexilic Judah and, later, on the synagogue and church. The next step will be to offer a brief history showing that xenophobia/nativism and misogyny are serious problems in the United States. The final step will be to reflect on the role and responsibility of the synagogues and churches with respect to these problems.

Introduction

THE HEBREW BIBLE INCLUDES a vast collection of protest literature of two types: protest against abuses that occurred before the Babylonian exile (586–538 BCE) and protest against abuses that occurred after this exile. This book focuses on the second type of protest. But before getting into a discussion of this second type, it is useful to say something about the first type.

The northern kingdom, Israel, from its earliest beginnings until its destruction by the Assyrian empire in 722 BCE, was a weak state oppressed by more powerful neighbors. The southern kingdom, Judah, was even weaker and was destroyed by the Babylonian empire at the beginning of the sixth century BCE. Not surprisingly, much of the Hebrew Bible's protest is directed against foreign enemies. After the Babylonian exile, the Jews[1] who had survived the Babylonian exile became monotheists, so that, when they edited the history of Israel and Judah—found in Deuteronomy through 2 Kings—they also protested vigorously against polytheism, against the Israelite or Judahite kings who had tolerated or even promoted polytheism, and against the social ills that they believed derive from polytheism. This first type of protest is found not only in Deuteronomy through 2 Kings but also in the books of the eighth-century

---

1. Scholars disagree about when the inhabitants of Judah can be called Jews, but the Hebrew word for "Jews" is the same as the Hebrew word for "inhabitants of Judah." Thus, in this book, the term "Jews" will be used to mean "anyone living in Judah." This term is not to be taken in a religious sense unless so specified.

Introduction

prophets, especially Amos, Hosea, and Micah, and in the books of the sixth-century prophets Jeremiah, Isaiah, and Ezekiel.

When the Babylonians destroyed Jerusalem and its temple, they forced Jerusalem's religious and literary elite into exile in Babylon. Fifty years later, upon returning to Jerusalem after the exile, this elite undertook the project of re-building the city walls and the temple but also, importantly, of converting the entire population of Judah to monotheism. In this monotheism project, Jewish intellectuals—whether those who had returned to Jerusalem or those who had chosen to remain in Babylon—were generally united, but as the project evolved, dissent arose over theological issues. The Hebrew Bible does not mention any such schism among Jewish intellectuals in the aftermath of the Babylonian exile, but the only plausible way to explain the production of texts like the books of Ruth, Jonah, and Job or the story of Rahab, which criticize key elements of the monotheism project, is to assume that Jewish intellectuals were divided into a very conservative main faction, who argued for a just and punitive God and who in this book will be referred to as the "hardliners," and one or more liberal factions, who argued for a gracious God and who will be called the "liberals." The second type of protest comes from these liberals. The aim of this book is to define God through an analysis of these liberal texts and to reflect on the relevance of that definition not only for postexilic Judah but also, and especially, for the modern world.

What gives these four liberal texts such importance is that, besides contributing to an understanding of God's grace, they underscore the fact that God has much more inclusive intentions than the hardliners ever imagined. That is, God loves and seeks to embrace all human beings—not only a particular ethnic group or gender. The message of these liberal texts is that the community and the world are blessed when, in imitation of God, the community lives by grace and rejects xenophobia, misogyny, and other forms of prejudice.

Because the northern kingdom was polytheistic and rife with corruption and with every form of social injustice, it is not surprising that protest arose against those abuses. Before the Babylonian exile, the southern kingdom was also polytheistic and corrupt, and that sad state of affairs produced a good deal of protest, too. But when the Jerusalem elite returned from exile in Babylon toward the end of the sixth century BCE, the situation in Judah improved dramatically. Specifically, the elite launched a program of religious purification and national unification based on loyalty to the one God and on worship in the re-built Jerusalem temple. This program was quite successful, as evidenced by the adoption and continuing vitality of monotheism among Jews in the postexilic period, roughly 538—350 BCE. Given this success, it seems reasonable to infer that this period was marked by a great meeting of the minds among Jews on matters both social and theological. However, as mentioned above, such was not the case. The best starting point for understanding why dissent arose is to explain the way that the hardliners viewed the history of Israel/Judah and the world.

The worldview of the hardliners was formed in Babylon, where they reflected on the destruction of Jerusalem and the temple—and on their own exile—and concluded that God was punishing them for centuries of polytheism. Extrapolating from that observation, the hardliners believed that the whole history of Israel followed the pattern set forth in the book of Judges—Israel sins, God punishes, Israel repents, and God forgives and rewards. Until sometime during the Babylonian exile, the Jerusalem elite had themselves been polytheistic, had wallowed in corruption and in all the other social diseases caused by the worship of false gods, and had been thoroughly disloyal to the God of Israel. It was the elite's exile experience that helped them—finally—to recognize the God of Israel as the one true God. Significantly, their exile experience also gave them a sense that they held the key to defining God. The elite came to believe that they deserved all the divine punishment that they had endured. But in Babylon they had sincerely repented and "paid their dues," so that now, according to the time-honored pattern of divine behavior, the hardliners believed that God was in turn forgiving them and blessing them.

Their safe return from exile, the successful reconstruction of the city walls and the temple, and the security they enjoyed under

Introduction

the protection of the Persian empire all seemed to confirm the understanding that the hardliners had of the way God operates in history. Moreover, in their view, the consistency with which God had followed this pattern of behavior—not only in their recent history but in the days all the way back to Noah—convinced them that this divine behavior was much more than a mere pattern; it was God's very nature. Thus, for the hardliners, God was above all a just and dependable God, whose behavior was predictable because God always acted according to the principle of punishing sinners and rewarding those who do good works. In other words, the hardliners believed in a God who repays good for good and evil for evil.[2] This was their definition of God. In this understanding of God, the rich are being rewarded by God for being good, and the poor are being punished for being sinners.

It was one thing for the hardliners to adopt such a theology themselves but quite another for them to induce the rest of the Jews to accept it. The hardliners had considerable prestige and influence among Judah's inhabitants, but these other Jews, amounting to about three-fourths of Judah's population, had never been exiled—had never had such a transformational experience—and thus had remained polytheists just as before the Babylonian exile. For this reason, there were important differences in attitude and opinion between those who had gone into exile and those who had remained in Judah. For example, the hardliners were motivated by a zealous desire to make all Jews practice exclusive loyalty to the God of Israel, understood as the God of retribution, lest the Jews sin again and invite another divine punishment. But many Jews, including some who had converted to monotheism, were understandably less enthusiastic, or simply had other ideas, the most important of which are developed in the four texts studied and which form the crux of the struggle to define God.

One fundamental idea came from polytheism. A polytheistic system provides gods for every problem or purpose and assumes that these gods can be propitiated by means of appropriate offerings and that all gods can be thus influenced. No god is thought to

2. Butterfield, 49–50.

Introduction

be so principle-bound and inflexible that he or she will not forgive and bless upon receipt of the right offering. To a polytheist, the notion of a god who is moralistic and judgmental, to the point of being impervious to propitiation and unfailingly committed to a policy of punishment, is very strange indeed. Thus, in postexilic Judah, whose history up until that time had been characterized by polytheism, the popular mind experienced a cognitive dissonance between already existing conceptions of gods and the predictably punitive God espoused by the hardliners. This was especially so since the idea of a gracious God, slow to anger and abounding in steadfast love, was not unknown among the Jews. Thus, even a Jew who had converted to monotheism might have cause to find fault with the theology of retribution, and many other Jews also had reason to dissent.

A more important reason for Jews to reject such a theology was the simple fact that the history of Israel and Judah was replete with examples of evil people who got rich and of good people who remained poor. Such a state of affairs was a clear contradiction of the theology of retribution, according to which God feels obliged to reward the good and to punish the bad. Hence even a casual observer of society could readily recognize that the theology of retribution was far from being a satisfactory definition or explanation of God.

The central objective of the hardliners was not only to practice their new religion themselves but, especially, to impose it upon the great mass of Jews, in order to make of them a cohesive community loyal to the one God, as the hardliners understood God. An important question, then, was how to build such cohesion, especially since many Jews had reason to remain indifferent or even to be actively uncooperative. One answer was for all the elite—not just the hardliners—to favor texts that pictured all people of Israelite/Judahite ethnicity as one big family. The patriarchal narratives, which depict all Israelites as descending from Abraham, provide just such a picture. Another answer was to educate, build group solidarity, and shape patterns of behavior. Celebration of the newly inaugurated liturgical festivals and of the Sabbath itself did exactly that. Still another answer was to promote commitment to the

Torah. Toward this end, the elite sponsored public readings from the Torah and urged the population to pledge allegiance to it.[3]

For centuries before the destruction of the Jerusalem temple by the Babylonians, the temple had been royal property dedicated to making round-the-clock sacrifices to a whole pantheon of gods, who, so ran the reasoning, had to be appeased in order to insure national security. Thus, the temple performed a governmental function and was not intended to attract or engage the average citizen. After the Babylonian exile, when the elite re-built the temple, they made the important political decision to re-brand the temple as the organizing center of national unity, a place for all Jews to congregate and celebrate.

But even with many government-sponsored activities designed to build solidarity and conformity, the elite in general found it difficult to make the Jews into a cohesive community that would be absolutely loyal to the God of Israel. The hardliners had even more trouble getting Jews to adopt the theology of retribution, especially because the hardliners felt that their theology required the banning of foreign wives. That policy seemed rather strange and harsh to most Jews, because they still thought of themselves mainly as what their name suggests—that is, as inhabitants of Judah—and for centuries the inhabitants of Judah had been free to marry whomever they pleased, including polytheists and women from any of the many and various ethnic groups that lived in or around Judah.

Not surprisingly, then, social tensions and dissent arose when the hardliners announced their plan to ban foreign wives in order to create a religiously pure community. Thus, women deemed "foreign" became the object of the hardliners' xenophobia. By "foreign," the hardliners meant "polytheistic" or "coming from an ethnic group whom they especially disliked." Labelling certain wives as foreign and banning them—even if those women had deep roots in Judah and had always been considered perfectly acceptable members of the community—was patently misogynist and xenophobic. Presumably, this policy of banning foreign wives

3. Ibid., 67–68.

INTRODUCTION

was hugely unpopular. It sought to ban wives and mothers who, it can well be imagined, were much loved by their family and friends and had much to contribute to the community. Hence, the decision to ban wives whom the hardliners deemed "foreign" was sure to produce a backlash.

Significantly, this policy singled out women as the cause of Israel's disloyalty to God and thus reflected a strong misogynist bias. By contrast, no matching policy was aimed at banning men who had polytheistic tendencies, even though men were capable of being every bit as disloyal to God as could women. This ban suggests that the hardliners viewed women as by nature particularly threatening and dangerous—a view of women that is in fact predominant in the Hebrew Bible. But, given that the northern kingdom was polytheistic throughout its history and that Judah was also polytheistic until sometime after the Babylonian exile, there was no political or religious justification for such a misogynistic policy until after the exile, when the hardliners decided to turn the project for monotheism into a project for religious and racial purity, too. Only then—and not before—did misogyny serve any political purpose. Thus, by implication, misogynist attitudes were introduced into the biblical literature by the hardliners.

The hardliners were also rather condescending. Ezra 4:1–3 implies that the hardliners considered themselves to be the sole arbiters of this new monotheism. The hardliners also sent their agents out beyond Jerusalem and into the diaspora in order to impose conformity on other Jews.[4] The power with which the hardliners imposed their views is best seen in the fact that they were able to make the theology of retribution predominant in the Hebrew Bible. Only the books of Jonah and Job present an alternative view. The hardliners felt superior, not only for being the privileged class in Jerusalem but also for having had the important experience of exile. Their hubris consisted especially in considering themselves to be the only ones who could define God and this new monotheism. Yes, God had spoken to them in Babylon, but they assumed

4. Schama, 40.

INTRODUCTION

that God had spoken only to them. Such absolutism and smugness virtually guaranteed dissent.

Thus, despite the conformity and unification usually associated with the period 538–350 BCE, it is really not surprising that considerable dissent arose against the theology and policies of the hardliners. What is surprising, however, is that this dissent assumed—not the form of riots and demonstrations—but the elegant form of great literature. The hardliners, it should be remembered, were quite adept at producing literature and were in fact responsible for the final form of Genesis through 2 Kings, as well as 1 and 2 Chronicles. There could not have been a more effective and appropriate way for dissenters to upstage, rebut, or educate the hardliners than to produce protest literature that in subtlety and refinement matched or even surpassed the literature produced by the hardliners.

The liberal literature to be explored in this book includes the following: the story of Rahab in Joshua 2 and the books of Job, Jonah, and Ruth—all of them works of extraordinary ingenuity and sophistication, and all dating from the postexilic period.

The objective of this exploration is, first, to show how these texts define God and how their definition of God influenced postexilic Judah, and then—importantly—to explain how their definition of God speaks to the current situation in the United States of America.

Ruth

Preliminary Remarks

The book of Ruth is relevant to this study, not only because it operates unhesitatingly on the assumption that God is indeed gracious, but also because it dramatically demonstrates God's desire to embrace all humankind. In both these ways, the book of Ruth reveals a God far different from the one pictured by the Jerusalem hardliners.

Ruth: Chapter 1

The story begins by claiming to be set in the period before the monarchy, the period of the so-called judges. Scholars agree, however, that it dates from postexilic Judah, most likely from the fourth century BCE. Biblical texts often pretend to be older than they really are because, in matters of religion, the Jews thought that older texts were more authoritative.

The action begins in Bethlehem, which is undergoing a famine. For this reason, an Israelite man, his wife, and two sons leave the country and go to Moab. To appreciate the significance of this choice of destinations, it is important to know that historically the Israelites had suffered much at the hands of several foreign countries, including the Edomites and the Egyptians, but that the Israelites had generally overcome their hatred of these two countries, as evidenced by Deuteronomy 23:8–9, which reads: "You shall not abhor an Edomite, for he is your kinsman. You shall not abhor an Egyptian, for you were a stranger in his land. Children born to them may be admitted into the congregation of the Lord in the third generation." Thus, descendants of the Edomites and the Egyptians are permitted to marry into Israel. But such is not at all the case with Moab or Ammon, which are the object of undying hatred among the Israelites, as evidenced by Deuteronomy 23:4–5, which reads: "No Ammonite or Moabite shall be admitted to the congregation of the Lord, because they did not meet you with food and water on your journey after you left Egypt, and because they hired Balaam son of Beor, from Pethor of Aram-naharaim, to curse you."

Thus, in the book of Ruth, an Israelite family goes to settle in a country that occupies a special place in the annals of Jewish xenophobia. Moab is the most enduringly and intensely despised of Israel's neighbors. Moab even hired a prophet to put a curse on the Israelites. Of course, the author of the book of Ruth chose Moab as the place where this Israelite family settles. The point is to make what follows all the more extraordinary. If something good can come out of Moab, the xenophobia of the hardliners in Jerusalem will be put to shame, and that is exactly the aim of this narrative.

The father of the Israelite family that settles in Moab is Elimelech; his wife is Naomi, and his two sons are Mahlon and Chilion. After they have settled in Moab, Elimelech dies and leaves Naomi with their two sons. The sons marry Moabite women, one named Orpah and the other Ruth. Ten years later, both sons die, so that Naomi is now without husband or sons or grandchildren. Thus, Naomi is in a precarious situation. She has no means of support, no property in Moab, and no family at all in Moab except for these two daughters-in-law, who are themselves widowed and thus also living precariously. Importantly, these women have no man to protect them, and for that reason all three have suffered a significant loss in social status. They are *déclassées* and defenseless.

Seeing no reason to remain in Moab, Naomi decides to return to Israel, because she has heard that God has put an end to the famine there. So, then, she sets out on the road to Bethlehem, accompanied by both Orpah and Ruth. But it soon occurs to Naomi that it would be unwise for Orpah and Ruth to leave their native country. Out of loving concern for her daughters-in-law, Naomi tells them to go back to their families of origin, and she asks God to deal kindly with them, just as they have dealt kindly with her and her two sons. The point is that, in the same way that it was wildly impractical for Israelites to settle in Moab, so it would be fruitless or even dangerous for Moabites to seek refuge in Israel. Thus, Naomi encourages Orpah and Ruth to stay in Moab and marry there. As she kisses them farewell, the daughters-in-law break into tears, saying: "No, we will return with you to your people." Note the possessive pronoun "your," which subtly reminds the reader of the awkward differences between Moabites and Israelites. Naomi is mindful of potential problems and thus urges Orpah and Ruth to go back home. Naomi employs the argument that she is too old to give them Israelite husbands again even if she married. Thus, these two young women need to think about marrying in Moab. More importantly, she says, it is not to their advantage to remain with her; her lot is worse than theirs, because the Lord has made it so. This last remark lends credence to the important suggestion that the God of Israel is at work orchestrating events.

Again, Orpah and Ruth break into tears. Then Orpah prudently decides to take Naomi's advice and bids her farewell, never to appear again in the narrative. But Ruth clings to Naomi, who, in response, affirms the wisdom of Orpah's decision and reiterates the estrangement that exists between Moabites and Israelites by saying that Orpah has returned to her people and to her gods and that Ruth should do likewise.

But Ruth replies, in words that over the centuries have lost none of their emotional and spiritual power: "Do not urge me to leave you, to turn back and not follow you. For wherever you go, I will go; wherever you lodge, I will lodge; your people shall be my people, and your God my God. Where you die, I will die, and there I will be buried. Thus and more may the Lord do to me if anything but death parts me from you."

With respect to this amazing statement, it is important that nothing in this story suggests that Ruth has become acculturated or converted to Israelite religion. In fact, both Naomi's statements and Ruth's have, up to this point, repeatedly shown an awareness that Israelite religion and culture are foreign to Ruth. Thus, when Ruth makes this surprising pledge to follow Naomi, to make Naomi's people her people, and Naomi's God her God, Ruth is acting in a counterintuitive manner that cannot be fully explained even by assuming the most exceptional personal loyalty or self-denial on Ruth's part. Ruth's decision is clearly designed to be a match for the totally unimaginable choice of Moab as a place for Israelites to settle. In other words, the only satisfactory explanation for Ruth's statement is that God has inspired it for God's own purposes, which presumably include providing for the welfare of these two widows but which may very well go far beyond that immediate objective. The reality is, then, that Ruth has not so much chosen Naomi and Naomi's God as that Naomi's God has chosen Ruth as his agent in a plan so far from human imagining that only God could have thought it up. Nevertheless, the existence of such a divine plan takes nothing away from Ruth's touching loyalty.

As for Ruth's remarkable pledge, her loyalty stands in sharp contrast to the disloyalty shown by Elimelech when he abandoned his community in a time of crisis. Remember that he left Bethlehem to escape a famine. Thus, in an ironic twist, the Moabite Ruth already reveals herself as more committed to the Israelite community than was the Israelite Elimelech. Only God's involvement with Ruth can plausibly explain her behavior. In fact, her loyalty to Naomi's God, whose hidden hand is at work behind the scenes, prefigures and explains everything that occurs later.

When the two widows arrive in Bethlehem, the whole city comes out to greet them. Women cry out, "Can this be Naomi?" But Naomi, whose name means "pleasantness," responds by telling people to call her Mara (bitterness), and she publicly blames the Lord for the bitterness she has experienced. She left Israel full but came back empty, she says, because the Lord had brought misfortune upon her. In this way, she publicized her need for the community's help and for God's.

Fortunately, Naomi returns to Bethlehem with Ruth at a most opportune time: the beginning of the barley harvest, which is the perfect opportunity for the community to help these hungry and defenseless widows. Since God is at work managing such details, there seems to be nothing coincidental about the timing of their arrival in Bethlehem.

Ruth: Chapter 2

In Moab, Naomi has no property and no kinfolk to help her, and so the first thing she does upon returning to Bethlehem is to publicly announce her indigent condition. In response to this appeal, the opening verses of this chapter offer a strong hint of promise. In Bethlehem, Naomi does indeed have kinfolk—specifically Boaz, a man related to her husband, a man of substance. Since Boaz is a kinsman of Elimelech, Boaz is most likely of Elimelech's generation and thus a mature adult.

Ever the hard-working and loyal companion, Ruth tells Naomi that she would like to glean among the ears of grain, working behind someone who may show her kindness. Notice how far from human imagining it is that Ruth, a just-arrived and still unprotected widow in a very strange land, should take the initiative and offer to go gleaning. Gleaning, interestingly, is not a Moabite practice and not something a Moabite would even know about. It is instead a distinctively Jewish idea enshrined in the Torah. That Ruth, a Moabite, should know about this legal provision and then, immediately and on her own initiative, want to glean, can plausibly be explained only if it is assumed again that Ruth is acting upon divine instruction. Verse 3 says that, "as luck would have it," the land where Ruth goes to glean belongs to Boaz. But, of course, luck has absolutely nothing to do with it.

One might well ask why this narrative makes it obvious, though never explicit, that God is at work behind the scenes, so that events correspond perfectly to God's will. This subtle technique speaks authoritatively to the intended audience, which is not only Jews in general but also, and especially, the hardliners in

Jerusalem. The purpose of this narrative is to change the hearts and minds of these hardliners, and that can be done only if they feel addressed by God.

In any case, Boaz soon arrives at his fields and greets his workers by saying, "The Lord be with you!" By any standard, this is a pious and loving way for a landowner to speak to his workers. Boaz treats them like family, and they respond in kind. Thus, we learn that Boaz is not only a man of substance but also a religious Jew who is full of community spirit and for whom the active presence of God among them is a given.

Because Boaz shows loving concern for his workers, he seems likely to show similar concern for this new girl working in his fields. "Whose girl is that?" he asks, and his men report that she is a Moabite girl who came back with Naomi from Moab and who asked to glean among the reapers. They then add a telling detail, namely, that this Moabite girl has been on her feet and working hard since early morning. This detail is designed to have an impact on Boaz, a community-minded Jew; he cannot be unmoved by this detail, which not only reveals Ruth's loyalty and energetic devotion to her mother-in-law—all the more wonderful because Ruth is a Moabite—but also reminds Boaz of his sacred obligation to defend the widow and the resident alien, Ruth being both widow and resident alien.

Boaz then speaks to Ruth in a fatherly and protective manner, as if she were his own daughter. Thus, we learn that Boaz takes his religious obligations quite seriously. He tells her not to glean in any other field, to stay close to his female workers, and to follow them. In a gesture of additional protection and hospitality, he orders his men not to molest her, and he invites Ruth to drink from his water supply whenever she is thirsty.

This scene shows how the divinely inspired behavior of Ruth, the impoverished Moabite widow and resident alien, is met with the divinely inspired response of Boaz, the religious Jew. Out of concern for the welfare of her mother-in-law, Ruth reaches out to the community for any help that the practice and legal principle of gleaning might offer her—and, in her gleaning, she spares no effort. Boaz, for his part, recognizes that it is his religious obligation to help her. He is not in the least deterred by the fact that she is a Moabite. In fact, her nationality only underscores the marvelous nature of her behavior and makes it all the more captivating. In this way, both Ruth and Boaz are counterintuitive characters. Who among the hardliners in Jerusalem would ever expect a Moabite to behave in a way so pleasing to the God of Israel? And who would expect a Jewish landowner living in this period marked by intense xenophobia to treat a Moabite with such loving kindness? This is only the first of several scenes designed to demonstrate that God calls us to exercise a radical hospitality in which there is no hint of xenophobia.

In fact, even Ruth recognizes how far from human imagining her situation is and so asks Boaz why he is being so kind as to single her out even though she is a foreigner. Boaz, who in this narrative is modeling the way the author wishes all Jews to behave, replies that he has been told about everything Ruth did for her mother-in-law—how Ruth left her mother and father and the land of her birth and came to a people she had not known before. In other words, Boaz both admires her loyalty to Naomi and appreciates the totally unexpected character of her decision and her behavior, which to him clearly indicate that this is God's handiwork and that Ruth is acting as God's agent. Thus, he responds by saying, "May the Lord reward your deeds. May you have full recompense from the Lord, the God of Israel, under whose wings you have sought refuge!"

Ruth's response to this blessing is ingenious: "You are most kind, my lord, to comfort me and to speak gently to your maidservant . . . " This show of respect for the stellar quality of Boaz as a religious Jew might have been enough to win his eternal loyalty. But she adds something even more suggestive and charming: " . . . even though I am not so much as one of your maidservants." This is an expression of the most sincere and abject humility, and no character trait is more valued among religious Jews—or by God—than humility. Boaz must have been mightily impressed. At the same time, Ruth's mention of the fact that she is not one of Boaz's kinfolk/family implies that Ruth could or should become a member of Boaz's family. Clearly, Ruth's hint does not fall on deaf ears either, because Boaz invites Ruth to join him and his kinfolk for lunch. Apparently, Ruth is given the honor of sitting near Boaz, because she is able to dip her bread in the same vinegar bowl that Boaz is using. Ruth eats her fill and, after the meal, has lots of leftovers to take home to Naomi.

As already pointed out, Boaz is playing the role of the exemplary religious Jew, but this status does not obviate the need for him to be prompted from time to time. Ruth's statement that she is not even one of his official maidservants is one such divinely inspired prompt.

When Ruth gets up from lunch in order to continue gleaning, Boaz takes his protective generosity to the next level by telling his workers to give her even more grain than she could possibly gather by gleaning. And, so, Ruth works until evening and ends up with a large amount of grain, which she then carries back to town. The sheer quantity of that grain, in addition to what was left over from Ruth's lunch with Boaz, impresses Naomi, who asks Ruth where she worked that day and, before even hearing Ruth's reply, offers a blessing on the person who was so generous to her.

Ruth explains that she worked with a man named Boaz. Naomi responds by blessing the Lord for his kindness to the living and the dead, a statement that Naomi immediately clarifies by explaining that Boaz is a relative of hers and thus qualifies as one of their redeeming kinsmen. This is an allusion to Leviticus 25:25, which reads: "If your kinsman is in straits and has to sell part of his holding, his nearest redeemer shall come and redeem what his kinsman has sold." It is also a reference to levirate marriage as spelled out in Deuteronomy 25:5—6, which reads: "When brothers dwell together and one of them dies, the wife of the deceased shall not be married to a stranger, outside the family. Her husband's brother shall unite with her: he shall take her as his wife and perform the levir's (redeemer's) duty. The first son that she bears shall be accounted to the dead brother, so that his name may not be blotted out in Israel." In other words, Boaz, as a kinsman of Elimelech, is one of those close male relatives who have a sacred legal responsibility to rescue Elimelech's name from oblivion by marrying Elimelech's widow, keeping ownership of Elimelech's land in the family, and fathering a son for Elimelech.

Ruth confirms the correctness of Naomi's impressions about Boaz by saying that he even told her to stay close to his workers throughout the harvest, a fact that both women interpret as a sign of Boaz's growing interest in and feeling of responsibility toward Ruth, who will take Naomi's place in this levirate marriage since Naomi is already too old.

Naomi encourages Ruth to follow Boaz's advice. So, then, Ruth gleans in Boaz's fields until the end of the barley harvest, after which she stays at home with her mother-in-law. Thus, everything is going according to plan, but the problem is that Boaz has not taken any further steps in Ruth's direction; he has yet to commit. Even though Boaz is an exemplary religious Jew, he still needs to be urged and prompted if the action of this divine plan is going to proceed.

Ruth: Chapter 3

Naomi now thinks of a way to push Boaz into making a commitment. She tells Ruth to bathe, dress up, and go down that very night to the threshing floor, where Boaz will be winnowing barley. When he has finished eating and drinking and has lain down to sleep, Ruth should uncover his feet and lie at the foot of his bed, at which point Boaz will tell Ruth what to do. Ruth promises to do as she is told.

Everything happens just as Naomi has instructed, so that in the middle of the night Boaz awakens to discover a woman lying at his feet. "Who are you?" he asks. Her response is bold and direct: "I am your handmaid Ruth." Note that she is no longer "not so much as one" of his maidservants; now she is most definitely his handmaid. Since Boaz has been so slow in taking the initiative, Ruth has had to take it for him and promote herself to handmaid. She then goes on to say, in a tone of voice that one may assume leaves little room for Boaz to hesitate or disagree, "Spread your robe over your handmaid, for you are a redeeming kinsman." Spreading his robe over her would be the official sign of his agreeing to marry her, and marrying her, she implicitly reminds him, is his sacred responsibility as a redeeming kinsman. Thus, Boaz gets pushed into action.

Because Boaz is a generation older than Ruth, this scene does not have all the sexual tension it would have if Boaz were a vigorous young man. In fact, Boaz exclaims, "Be blessed of the Lord, daughter! Your latest deed of loyalty is greater than the first, in that you have not turned to younger men, whether rich or poor." What Boaz means, apart from simply thinking of Ruth as his daughter, is that Ruth was loyal to Naomi once by staying with her and gleaning for her and then a second time by seeking—not a young lover such as a young woman like Ruth might prefer—but an older man who could rescue Naomi and redeem Elimelech's name.

In this story, Boaz has experienced quite a remarkable journey. In his very first encounter with Ruth, he is greatly impressed with her hard work and her devotion to her mother-in-law, and, since both women are defenseless widows, he feels a strong religious obligation to help them, especially Ruth, who is also a resident alien. Ruth, for her part, displays personal qualities that would be striking in any girl but that in a Moabite are preternatural and suggest divine inspiration. Boaz has warm fatherly feelings toward Ruth and is also moved by her genuine humility and loyalty and by her courageous decision to leave Moab and come to a place she did not know. He senses that God is at work through Ruth, but he is not yet sure exactly what his own role is in this divine-human drama. But Boaz finds at least one action to be immediately appropriate: to ask God to bless Ruth. And, so, Boaz does.

Now, wanting to be closer to Ruth and to help her even more, he invites her into his kinship circle and treats her with great fatherly generosity. He is still not sure, though, where this relationship should go from there. But Naomi, presumably with God's help, has already solved this problem. On the threshing floor in the middle of the night, Ruth gives Boaz the divinely ordained answer: he must exercise his responsibility as a redeeming kinsman and marry Ruth. Already aware of such legal responsibilities and eager to learn exactly what his role will be, Boaz is not surprised by what Ruth tells him in the middle of the night. In fact, he welcomes the news and tells Ruth to have no fear. He will do whatever she asks, because, he says, everyone knows what a fine woman she is. But, of course, he is also motivated by the realization that what Ruth said to him on the threshing floor is not merely a suggestion but really a command from God.

Boaz's motivation to act henceforth is thus a sweet blend of admiration and respect for Ruth, desire to fulfill the *mitzvah* of defending widows and resident aliens, and obedience to the specific command that God gave him through Ruth on the threshing floor. Boaz is absolutely exhilarated to learn that God has chosen him to consummate God's plan for Naomi and Ruth. He knows that such a plan will indeed help Naomi and Ruth, but, precisely because Ruth is a Moabite, this plan is replete with repercussions far beyond the welfare of two widows. Boaz is thrilled to understand—finally—what's going on and to know that he now plays the key role in the drama. As a result, he feels tremendously empowered.

Boaz realizes, however, that there is an important obstacle to his carrying out this plan. He is indeed a redeeming kinsman, but another redeeming kinsman is even more closely related than Boaz. He promises to speak to the other, closer redeemer in the morning and find out what the other man will do. Meanwhile he invites Ruth to stay at the threshing floor until dawn, but, in order to avoid any gossip that might interfere with consummation of the plan, he makes sure that Ruth leaves before sunrise, so that no one will know that she was there. As she prepares to leave, he gives her a weighty amount of grain to take back to Naomi. When Ruth arrives home, Naomi tells her to relax and wait patiently because, knowing men as she does—especially religious Jews zealous to act in partnership with God—she is sure that Boaz will settle the matter immediately.

Ruth: Chapter 4

Meanwhile, Boaz goes to the city gate, where trials or transactions requiring witnesses usually take place, and when the other, closer redeemer—who is unnamed in the story—walks by, Boaz calls him over and tells him to sit down. Then Boaz summons ten elders as witnesses and explains the situation to the other redeemer. He says that Naomi has returned from Moab and must sell a piece of land that belonged to their kinsman Elimelech. Boaz explains that the other man is a redeeming kinsman closer to Elimelech than is Boaz. Thus, if the other man wants to redeem that piece of land, he should do so now in the presence of the witnesses. In fact, the other man does want to redeem that piece of land. But then Boaz explains that if the other man acquires the property belonging to Naomi and Ruth, he must also acquire the wife of the deceased, so that the name of the deceased will remain on the property. Whether Ruth or Naomi is intended as the wife is not clear. In any case, upon learning of this condition attached to acquisition of the land, the other redeemer gives up his right of redemption because it would impair his estate. That is, he would have to share his estate with whatever son was produced in this levirate marriage.

Interestingly, this other redeemer is not named—and it must be assumed that this failure to name him is intentional—no doubt because he represents the hardliners, whom this narrative is addressing in an attempt to convince them to do God's will concerning foreigners. The implication is that, out of a mixture of self-interest and xenophobia, the hardliners are obstructing God's will with their policy of banning foreign wives and, what's worse, are refusing to be a blessing to the nations. For this reason, the hardliners deserve to be nameless. At this point, remember how important it is to maintain one's name in Israel. If one's name falls into oblivion, as was the danger in Elimelech's case, then one ceases to be part of Israel. Thus, the failure to grant a name to this other redeemer is a subtle technique for telling the hardliners what could happen to them; it is a way of scaring them and touching them on a very deep and sensitive level. By contrast, God's faithful partners—the true Israel—are represented by Naomi, Ruth, and Boaz, who, importantly, all have names.

To dramatize and solemnize this transaction at the city gate, the other redeemer, as a sign that he is giving up his right of redemption, hands his sandal to Boaz. Boaz, in turn, shows the sandal to the elders and announces that he himself is acquiring from Naomi all that belonged to Elimelech and all that belonged to Mahlon and Chilion, and that he is also acquiring Ruth the Moabite, wife of Mahlon, to be his own wife, in order to perpetuate the name of the deceased upon his estate, so that the name of the deceased may not disappear from among his kinsmen. Boaz concludes by calling all the people at the city gate to witness.

The witnesses are obviously pleased, because they respond, "We are witnesses!" As a further sign of their delight with Boaz's announcement, they ask God to make the woman coming into Boaz's house as fruitful as Leah and Rachel, who built up the house of Israel. Note that associating Ruth with the likes of Leah and Rachel is already a high honor. They also ask that God perpetuate Boaz's name in Bethlehem and make his house like the house of Perez, whom Tamar bore to Judah (Genesis 38) and from whom the Davidic kings descend.

The joyful community spirit of the townspeople in this scene is remarkable. It is as if the consummation of the divine plan has brought out the best in their Jewishness, so that they immediately recognize the exercise of Boaz's right of redemption as a great blessing on the current and future community.

And so, Boaz marries Ruth. He is old and probably past the age of procreation, but God lets Ruth conceive, and she bears a son, who will be called Obed (servant) because Naomi, Ruth, and Boaz have been such faithful servants of God and because, they hope, Obed will also serve God. The women of the town rejoice with Naomi, bless the Lord for providing her with a redeemer, ask God to perpetuate the redeemer's name, and assure Naomi that she will be sustained in her old age, all because this child was born of her daughter-in-law, who loves her more than seven sons. Note that it is the women of the town who draw the appropriate conclusion from what has happened—namely, that a wonderful blessing has come to Naomi and to Israel because of a Moabite girl. Thus, not only is xenophobia marked as contrary to God's will and as a failure of Israel's responsibility to be a blessing to the nations, but the community that rejects xenophobia and welcomes the resident alien into its family—no matter where that alien comes from—receives a great blessing. That is the over-arching moral of this story.

The people who were at the city gate and the women around Naomi understand that what has happened between Ruth and Boaz is God's benevolent doing, and thus no hint of doubt or xenophobia spoils the people's joy. In this way, the townspeople also display the attitude that the author hopes all Jews will have toward foreigners.

To emphasize the selflessness and humility of Ruth's role in this drama, as well as the wholesome effect that her actions have on the community, the narrative focuses now—not on Ruth—but on Naomi, who takes the baby in her arms and becomes its foster mother, so that the women neighbors refer to the baby as Naomi's. But then the focus subtly shifts back to Ruth when, in fulfillment of the hope that the people expressed at the city gate, Ruth's baby enters the line of Perez, from whom the kings of Judah descend. This happens because Boaz is a direct descendant of Perez. Thus, the Moabite widow Ruth not only marries into the people of God but will become the great-grandmother of King David.

In this way, the narrative ends with a nicely balanced, community-minded emphasis on both Naomi and Ruth and on Israel itself, while Boaz is not forgotten either since his name appears in the concluding genealogy.

The Relevance of the Book of Ruth for Postexilic Judah

Throughout the postexilic period, the hardliners consistently maintained their policy forbidding marriage with foreigners. The hardliners never changed their mind on this issue. Because they considered idolatry to be the single gravest threat to Judah's existence as the people of God, and because they associated idolatry with foreigners, particularly women, they held to their policy. Without such a policy, they believed, the religiously pure community they were seeking to build would not have been possible.

The counterargument, as implied in the book of Ruth, is that the policy of banning foreigners would have the effect of cloistering the new monotheistic community and that such self-ghettoization would fly in the face of some of the most cherished tenets of the new monotheism—namely, that the God of Israel is the God of all creation and loves all human beings, and that Israel's assignment as the people of God is to be a blessing to all the nations. The message of the book of Ruth is also that God may choose to partner with foreigners, so that the divine blessing may very well flow from the nations to Israel. Thus, the liberals felt that the policy against foreign wives represented disobedience to God's will and would have all sorts of negative consequences. It would even distort the people's understanding of God and thus vitiate their role as God's agents in history.

What is highly instructive about the book of Ruth is that, by calmly presenting its audience with the vision of a more excellent way of treating foreigners—rather than making a direct rational argument against xenophobia—the liberals acknowledge, implicitly, that the hardliners are not open to rational argument on this subject. The liberals understand that the hardliners are not going to change their minds unless tricked into it. Thus, in telling the story of Ruth, the liberals look for some hook to "catch the conscience of the king," some leverage to force the hardliners to change. But, since the hardliners hold all the power in Judah, the liberals have no choice but to manufacture some leverage, which consists in the implied threat that, if the hardliners insist on acting more like the closer redeemer—who rejects the foreigner—than like Boaz—who marries her—they will end up nameless, forgotten, and thus no longer Israel. This was a bold and desperate attempt to convert the hardliners, but, historically, it failed for lack of sufficient leverage.

Although the story of Ruth did not achieve its desired results in postexilic Judah, it remains an inspiring demonstration of God's will toward the other. The other in this story is someone so despised and so different that Boaz, the sincerely religious Jew, must focus entirely on God's will and exclude all competing thoughts.

Thus, the enduring value of the book of Ruth seems to center on the figure of Boaz, who demonstrates what it means to be loyal to the God of Israel. Boaz meets a woman whom his society is conditioned to hate and fear, but, loyal to God, he treats her with warm, fatherly generosity and total acceptance. Furthermore, Boaz does so with spontaneity and eagerness, which show how he delights in being God's faithful servant. He may have to be pushed and prompted occasionally, but his heart is always in the right place. In this way, he becomes a model of faithfulness for succeeding generations of Jews and Christians.

Significantly, Boaz's kinfolk and the townspeople seem to understand what Boaz is doing, and just as Ruth's joy in remaining loyal to Naomi is contagious and sparks joy in Boaz, so Boaz's joy in serving God generates joy in all the people around him. As the ending makes clear, this is not a transient or inconsequential joy, either, because it leads to a substantial blessing, not only for Naomi, Ruth, Boaz, and the town of Bethlehem but for all Israel. The message is that, if only Israel could follow the example of Boaz, who opened himself in love to a foreigner, Israel would be blessed. In light of the fact that the hardliners rejected this message, however, the book of Ruth might now be thought of also as a reflection on opportunities lost. And yet, since this story is told in such a way that, at every step, the action is the unfolding of God's will, this story demands to be taken seriously.

Jonah

Preliminary Remarks

The book of Jonah contributes to the struggle to define God through its depiction of God as consistently behaving contrary to the theology of retribution.

Jonah: Chapter 1

In the opening line of this narrative, the protagonist's name immediately attracts attention. Jonah, in Hebrew *Yonah*, means "dove" and thus points back to the role of the dove in the story of Noah (see especially Genesis 8), where the dove heralds the end of the great flood that God used to destroy a sinful humanity and marks the beginning of the re-creation that God aims to perform through Noah's sons. This dove imagery can be taken to mean that, in the Jonah story, God is planning another destruction/re-creation by water. What kind of destruction/re-creation it might be is hinted at by Jonah's family name, *Amittai*, which is based on the root *emeth* (truth). The implication is that Jonah will be the herald of some truth.

As suggested above, the name Jonah calls to mind the important biblical imagery not only of destruction by water but also of divine blessing in the form of separation from water, such as occurs in creation (Genesis 1:6–10), in the Noah story, in the account of Moses' birth (Exodus 2), and in the exodus from Egypt (Exodus 14).

The Struggle to Define God

The word that comes from the Lord is for Jonah to go at once to Nineveh and proclaim judgment upon the city, because God has become aware of the wickedness of the Ninevites. It is useful to know that Nineveh was the capital of the Assyrian empire, which included the city of Babylon, that the Assyrian empire was responsible for the destruction of the northern kingdom, and that the Babylonian empire, which replaced the Assyrian, was later responsible for the destruction of Jerusalem, including the temple, and for the deportation of Jerusalem's elite citizenry to Babylon. As a result, the name Nineveh represents the most horrific atrocities that the Israelites ever endured. Although Israel's prophets looked upon these atrocities as well-deserved divine chastisement for Israel's worship of false gods, it is also true that this chastisement was so exceedingly harsh and cruel that the Israelites would naturally expect the Assyrians and Babylonians to receive some divine punishment, too, especially because the dominant theology of this narrative's intended audience in postexilic Judah favored the theology of retribution, according to which God always punishes evil-doers and rewards those who do good.

Thus, when Jonah learns that he is supposed to pronounce judgment on Nineveh, he should be delighted to get this assignment, but instead he flees from the Lord's service. Traditionally, though Israel's prophets were often somewhat reluctant to serve, they never actually fled from the Lord's service. Jonah's action is therefore unprecedented. The most plausible explanation is that he is a strong supporter of the theology of retribution but must somehow be convinced that the Lord will not conform to that theology's rules for God's conduct and thus that the Lord might very well not punish Nineveh for its unpardonable sins. In short, Jonah suspects that God finds the theology of retribution unacceptable, but Jonah stubbornly advocates for it nevertheless.

Certainly, all the above suggests that this narrative must have been written by someone who opposes the theology of retribution, a writer who makes Jonah the spokesperson for that theology and who expresses his opposition to it through the character called the Lord. As the narrative continues, it is important that, no matter how much the author may disagree with Jonah or how bizarre Jonah's behavior may be, Jonah retains a certain dignity as the advocate for a very respectable point of view; Jonah believes in the importance of a moral universe, that is, one in which good people are rewarded, and the guilty are punished. If God does not feel constrained by this principle of rewarding the good and punishing the guilty—and Jonah is afraid that such is the case—the result, Jonah thinks, will be a universe that is not moral. And a universe that is not moral is chaos. Thus, when Jonah flees from the Lord, he is actually fleeing in protest of the chaos he believes will ensue if God is unwilling to punish those egregious sinners in Nineveh.

In Jonah's attempt to flee, he boards a ship bound for Tarshish, an exotic name that suggests a faraway place; Jonah wants to get as far away as possible. But a great tempest comes upon the sea, and the ship is in danger of breaking up. In ancient Near Eastern mythology, the sea is the domain of the chaos monster Moth (Death), and a storm is the visible sign of Moth's power. In Genesis 1:1–2, God imposes a certain control over Moth's power, but that control is far from permanent or complete, so that from time to time Moth can still cause serious trouble. Yet, in this case, God chooses to stand by and allow trouble to happen. Thus, this storm is an indirect way for God to speak to Jonah. The message is that if Jonah believes that anything short of a perfectly moral universe is chaos, God will show him, by means of this storm, what real chaos looks like. Hence the storm is God's teaching moment.

As the storm worsens, the ship's crew panics and begins throwing cargo overboard. Meanwhile, Jonah has gone below deck and fallen asleep. What is Jonah trying to prove? It seems plausible to suggest that, by sleeping and thus ignoring the storm, Jonah is trying to tell the Lord that he has not been intimidated by the Lord's show of force and is not afraid and—importantly—that he has not budged from his insistence on a moral universe. Jonah seems unshakable in defense of this principle.

When the captain comes to wake up Jonah, he tells Jonah that he should call upon his god and beg for mercy. Apparently, the captain and crew are more impressed by this display of divine power than is Jonah. The men cast lots to determine on whose account this storm arose, and the lot falls to Jonah. The men want to know who Jonah is, where he comes from, and of what people. Jonah tells them that he is a Hebrew and that he worships the Lord, God of Heaven, who made the sea and the land. The men immediately realize that the cause of this storm is that Jonah has done something to displease the Lord, and they are terrified. When they discover that Jonah has attempted to flee from the service of the Lord, they ask him what they should do to calm the sea. Then, in an act that reveals Jonah's stubborn determination to resist the Lord's show of force, to defend the principle of a moral universe, and—importantly—to reject the very possibility that the people of Nineveh could be pardoned, Jonah tells them to throw him into the sea. This solution, however, is so radical and heartless that the men refuse to obey and attempt instead to row to shore, but they discover that they cannot do so. As the storm intensifies, the men pray that the Lord not let them perish on account of Jonah and—amazingly—that the Lord not hold them guilty of killing an innocent person because "you, O Lord, by your will, have brought this about." They then throw Jonah overboard, and the storm ceases. The men, who fear the Lord greatly, make vows, the exact nature of which is left unspecified, and the scene ends abruptly.

The irony of this episode is that the captain and crew, none of whom are Israelites, respond to the Lord exactly as the Lord would like Jonah to respond—namely, with respect and awe. They also beg for mercy, in effect, on a certain theological basis. The Lord should not let them, who are obviously innocent, perish because of Jonah. This appeal to the Lord's justice conforms with the theology of retribution. But they also tell the Lord that Jonah is innocent, because the Lord himself is the maker of the storm and the origin of this whole problem. The effect of this argument is, on the one hand, to support the theology of retribution: those who have not done evil should not be punished. But, on the other hand, these men ask the Lord to consider Jonah innocent, even though Jonah has stubbornly, even proudly, chosen to be guilty and has admitted his guilt. Thus, this appeal for clemency for Jonah is made—not on the basis of the theology of retribution—but on the basis of divine grace. That is, in defense of Jonah, the sailors have recourse to exactly the theology that Jonah refuses to accept, namely, the theology of grace.

In this clever way, the author manages, while showing some respect for the theology of retribution, to introduce its polar opposite—namely, the idea that the Lord is capable of graciously ignoring Jonah's guilt and declaring him innocent. God has that freedom; God is gracious. That this idea should come from the mouth of Gentile sailors expresses another insight near and dear to liberal texts in the Hebrew Bible—namely, that Gentiles sometimes understand the Lord better than do the Israelites.

In any case, the sailors finally throw Jonah overboard, and the storm ceases.

Jonah: Chapter 2

Jonah is now in the water, which is the lair of Moth, and thus is exposed to the power of death/chaos. The Lord responds indirectly to Jonah—not on the basis of retribution, since Jonah is guilty—but on the basis of grace, by providing a big fish to swallow Jonah. This fish rescues Jonah from the water and protects him from the power of Moth. For three days, Jonah remains in the belly of the fish, which is swimming in what is definitely Moth's territory, and thus Jonah is protected but also decidedly trapped. Jonah has been saved from death but held prisoner in a place that in every respect is far from the Lord. Remember that, by boarding a ship bound for Tarshish, Jonah showed that he wanted to be far from the Lord. Well, now he is.

What is the Lord attempting to accomplish with this rescue and three-day imprisonment? Is it the Lord's intention to make Jonah experience up close just what real chaos is like? Apparently, yes. The implicit message from the Lord is that stubborn disobedience to the Lord distances Jonah from the Lord, and that this estrangement is itself chaos. Jonah's experience in the belly of the fish seems intended to teach him that the price to be paid for his defending a noble but false understanding of God is alienation from God, a result equivalent to never getting out of the fish's belly. The fact that the Lord has rescued Jonah from the water indicates that the Lord is indeed gracious—not acting in accordance with the theology of retribution—and that he expects Jonah to emerge transformed from the belly of the fish, and to carry out his assigned mission. Jonah, for his part, thinks that he now understands what the Lord meant by the storm and the fish. Thus, in the belly of the fish, he prays and reflects on his experience, the details of which are quite revealing.

Jonah begins by saying that, from the hell in which he found himself, he called out to the Lord, and the Lord answered him. This statement reveals that he understands at least what it meant to be trapped in the belly of the fish. It represented isolation from God, and such is the definition of hell. But it is not yet clear what Jonah means when he says that the Lord heard his voice and answered hm. He is, after all, still in the belly of the fish, and no communication between Jonah and the Lord has occurred during Jonah's three days there. However, the next portion of his prayer offers some clarity.

Jonah says that it was the Lord who cast him into the depths and made him sink to the bottom, where he thought he'd never again see the temple in Jerusalem, and that it was the Lord who brought him up because Jonah's prayer had risen before the Lord in the temple. Thus, with loud thanksgiving, Jonah says, he will sacrifice to the Lord, who is responsible for his deliverance. Note that Jonah's prayer is in the past tense, as if Jonah were so sure that what he asks for will happen that he can already talk about it as past.

This prayer reveals that, though the Lord intended Jonah's time in the belly of the fish to be a learning experience and though Jonah thinks he has learned his lesson, in fact, he has not learned, because he pictures his sinking as punishment, his prayer as repentance, and the Lord's bringing him up as the response that the theology of retribution requires of God. The experience of rescue from the water was meant to teach him the theology of grace, but all it succeeded in doing was confirming his trust in the theology of retribution. The Lord was attempting to transform Jonah, but Jonah remains unchanged.

Jonah knows that he is guilty of failing to accept his mission and instead of attempting to flee from the Lord. Yet, in Jonah's mind, these are minor offenses in light of what Jonah considers his heroic defense of the theology of retribution, which, for Jonah—and for the hardliners in Jerusalem—is a sacred principle. Jonah imagines himself as nobly resisting the Lord in a courageous attempt to make the Lord be true to himself. Whatever punishment Jonah may have received, he naturally considers unjust. Thus, he is grateful for the Lord's help, but he also believes that the Lord is obligated to deliver heroes like him. Jonah also has the idea that his prayer somehow obliges God to deliver him. After all, the Lord is, Jonah says, the Deliverer. Hence Jonah is thankful for what the Lord will do, but he believes that his deliverance will be only what the Lord, by virtue of being the Deliverer, will have to do anyway. From this same tit-for-tat perspective, Jonah now feels obliged to make the appropriate sacrifices in the temple. In short, Jonah still clings to the theology of retribution.

In any case, the Lord commands the fish, and it spits Jonah back onto dry land.

Jonah: Chapter 3

Being every bit as stubborn as Jonah, the Lord commands him a second time to go to Nineveh and proclaim judgment upon it. This time Jonah obeys, perhaps out of fear of being sent back into the belly of the fish. Arriving in Nineveh, he walks through the city, proclaiming that in forty days the Lord will overthrow the city unless the people repent.

Just as Jonah feared, the people of Nineveh believe the Lord. They proclaim a feast and put on sackcloth as a sign of repentance. Even the king of Nineveh puts on sackcloth and sits in ashes as an even greater sign of repentance. In fact, the king declares a general fast that includes not only people but their flocks and herds. He also decrees that all living beings in Nineveh must cry out mightily to the Lord and turn from their evil ways, so that the Lord may turn back from his wrath.

As a result of Nineveh's repentance, the Lord renounces the punishment he was planning to carry out and thus acts in a way contrary to the theology of retribution, which would require that the people of Nineveh, well-nigh-unpardonable sinners that they are, be punished before being eventually forgiven.

Jonah: Chapter 4

The Lord's decision greatly displeases Jonah, who prays to the Lord, saying that such divine clemency is exactly what he anticipated when the Lord first commanded him to go to Nineveh; it's what made him flee to Tarshish. Jonah adds, resignedly, that he knows the Lord is a compassionate and gracious God, slow to anger, abounding in kindness, and renouncing punishment. But, of course, this reality is exactly what Jonah wishes he didn't know, exactly what he wishes were not true, because, with such a God, the wicked—and none were more wicked than the Ninevites—go unpunished. Thus, with a forgiving God like this, the universe is not moral, and an immoral universe is chaos—the equivalent to death. Hence Jonah begs the Lord to take his life. He would rather die than live in a universe that is not moral.

The Lord's response to Jonah is revealing. God asks, "Are you that deeply grieved?"—a question that has a number of implications. First, it suggests that Jonah has established a false equivalence between life and the theology of retribution, as if life simply could not go on if that particular understanding of God did not prevail. When the Lord graciously put Jonah into the protective custody of the fish's belly, in spite of Jonah's obvious guilt, the Lord was trying to teach him that God is above all gracious and that life means nearness to God. In the fish's belly, which was far from God, Jonah was expected to realize how crucial it is to be near to God.

Being gracious, God is in no way obligated to punish the guilty; God is free to pardon them, no matter how unpardonable they may seem to Jonah. If that were not true, the Lord would have been obliged to let the guilty man Jonah drown. Clearly, despite all of Jonah's gratitude to God and his professed understanding of the situation, he has not learned the basic lesson—namely, that decisions about punishment and forgiveness belong strictly to God, who is free to decide as God sees fit.

Second, the Lord's question implies that Jonah is behaving in an intrusive and foolish manner when he presumes to tell the Lord how to be God. The Lord seems to be saying, "Jonah, haven't you forgotten who's God around here?" Or, "Sure, Jonah, the theology of retribution is predominant in the Torah and with the hardliners in Jerusalem, but does that mean that I, the Lord, have to let myself be confined by that theology? Aren't you making the mistake of loving your theology more than you love me?"

Finally, the Lord's question suggests that, in the Lord's opinion, Jonah has enough problems of his own, without fretting over the Lord's decisions. If being alive means being near to God, Jonah should be more concerned about his own situation, because Jonah has let his obsession with the theology of retribution distance himself from God and become a barrier between them.

In any event, Jonah leaves Nineveh, goes to a nearby hill where he makes a booth from which he can observe what's happening in the city, and then sits down in the shade. The Lord graciously provides a plant to help shade Jonah and save him from discomfort, and Jonah is in fact happy to have this plant. But the next day the Lord also provides a worm that attacks the plant and makes it wither, so that after sunrise the wind and sun grow hot on Jonah's head.

This plant is obviously another gracious gift from the Lord, but Jonah does not acknowledge it as such. Instead he takes the Lord's gift for granted. Therefore, the Lord takes back the gift, and the loss of this plant, which Jonah thinks the Lord owed him for carrying out his mission, only reinforces Jonah's conclusions: that the universe has indeed devolved into chaos, that there is no justice, that the Lord is not acting like God, that the universe is not moral, and that, given such chaos, Jonah might as well be dead. Thus, when Jonah becomes faint from the sun, he begs again for death.

The Lord's response this time is the same as before: "Are you really so grieved about the plant?" Which is to say, "Are your priorities still so confused? Are you still unable to understand anything about me?"

Jonah remains a stout defender of the theology of retribution, and his stubbornness constitutes the main obstacle to his relationship with the Lord. It blinds Jonah to his own alienation from the Lord and makes it impossible for him to be alive in the sense of being near to God. And since Jonah presumably represents the views of the Jerusalem hardliners, the author of this narrative is saying that the supposedly infallible arbiters of the new monotheistic orthodoxy in Jerusalem are, like Jonah, alienated from God and thus spiritually dead, and, what's worse, remain totally blind to that fact.

In the closing verses of this story, the Lord summarizes Jonah's problem by saying that even Jonah cared about the shade plant, which was pure grace, even if Jonah did not recognize it as such. So much more, then, should the Lord care about all those many Ninevites who did recognize and appreciate the Lord's grace.

Thus, this narrative represents a contest of wills between equally stubborn but otherwise unevenly matched opponents. Jonah, the lesser of the two competitors, tries vainly to impose upon the Lord a certain widely accepted but fundamentally incorrect view of who the Lord is and how the Lord acts. Throughout the contest, Jonah receives all the respect due to someone who espouses the noble desire for a moral universe, but, repeatedly failing to understand that the Lord does not feel compelled to play by Jonah's rules, Jonah effectively distances himself from the Lord. Meanwhile, the Lord never stops offering Jonah opportunities for appreciating the Lord's gracious nature. Even at the conclusion of the narrative, the Lord still believes that Jonah is capable of grasping this concept called grace.

Thus, this narrative manages to give a respectful, gentle, generous, but thoroughly devastating rebuttal of the theology of retribution, while opening the audience's mind to the theology of grace. In this way, a principle that the Jerusalem hardliners considered to be absolutely true—the theology of retribution—is refuted, so that the truth about God can emerge. This constitutes a destruction/re-creation of ideas, and in this case the ideas are ones that affect the believer on the deepest level.

Despite the fact that the Jerusalem hardliners, who had editorial authority over Hebrew texts, rejected the theology of grace, it should be clear that it is, nevertheless, profoundly Jewish. Given the political power that the hardliners exercised, it is surprising that that the book of Jonah survived long enough to be included eventually in the Hebrew Bible, and even more surprising that this book became the text for Yom Kippur, when Jews ask God to judge them. It seems that the Jews decided that they would rather be judged by a gracious God than by a God who insisted on punishing them first.

It should also be pointed out that the theology of grace, as seen in this narrative, does not necessarily exclude the possibility of a moral universe at all. God has no obligation to punish sinners, but God is perfectly free to chastise them for educational purposes and transform them. In this way, God's justice and God's mercy can amount to much the same thing.

Overall, this narrative shows that God is free to an extent that Jonah—and the hardliners for whom he speaks—strongly disavowed. The fact that such a text eventually came to play a prominent role in Jewish worship is a parade example of the positive impact that a dissenting text can eventually have on the community for which it was written.

The Relevance of the Book of Jonah in Postexilic Judah

Apart from the obvious fact that this book demonstrates its opposition to the theology of retribution and favors the theology of grace, it is clear that, since Jonah represents the Jerusalem hardliners, this story does an effective job of putting that elite in its place. They are treated with respect and receive grace upon grace, but they reveal themselves, at the same time, to be alienated from God and, finally, rather pathetic. The inference to be drawn is that the author of this book is trying—not to destroy the hardliners—but to shame them into reforming their theology.

The book of Jonah also offers a radical challenge to the ethnocentrism of the hardliners, who never could have imagined sharing God's tent with foreigners, especially Ninevites. Neither could the hardliners have ever imagined that Gentile sailors would know more about God than they did. In this story, God is seen drawing the Gentile world to himself, while, back in Judah, the hardliners are attempting to ban foreign wives.

In all these ways, the book of Jonah shows that the supposed leaders of postexilic Judah, the self-appointed arbiters of monotheism, are as much opponents of God as they are proponents of monotheism. The ones who claim to speak for God are shown to be those who most need to be re-educated by God. Thus, the book of Jonah makes a subtle but devastating critique of Judah's leaders and of their theology, while presenting a much more powerful and appealing theology—namely, the theology of grace.

Job

Preliminary Remarks

The book of Job reveals God as free, unfettered, and not bound by the pattern of divine behavior set forth in the theology of retribution, which is rejected as mere human invention.

Job: Chapter 1

The story of Job begins by providing some important information—namely, that the action takes place—not in Israel, but in a foreign location called Uz, so that Job, the protagonist, is presumably a Gentile. Job is blameless and upright; he fears God and shuns evil. In this way, the author says implicitly but succinctly that God also operates actively outside Israel and that it is quite possible for a Gentile to be blameless and upright. In the space of only one verse, the author rejects the ethnocentric, xenophobic point of view of the dominant faction of the Jerusalem elite.

Job, who has seven sons and three daughters, possesses many sheep, camels, oxen, and asses, as well as a large household. He is the richest man in the whole region. It is the custom of Job's sons to hold feasts, and, after each one, Job advises his sons to sanctify themselves, while he makes burnt offerings for them, just in case they have sinned or blasphemed God. Without any doubt, then, Job is both sinless and scrupulously loyal to God.

One day, the Adversary (aka Satan), whose role is to test people's loyalty, comes before God, who asks him if he has seen

Job. For good reason, God is very proud of Job, but the Adversary suggests that Job is loyal and pious only because God has made him rich and that, if God took away Job's possessions, Job would surely blaspheme God. God takes this bet and gives the Adversary permission to do whatever he likes, provided he does not harm Job physically.

Acting with a free hand, the Adversary arranges to have all Job's possessions stolen and all his children murdered. Job tears his robe in a sign of mourning, throws himself on the ground, worships God, and piously proclaims that because everything he had was a gift from God, God has every right to take it back. In so doing, Job remains perfectly loyal to God.

Job: Chapter 2

When the Adversary comes before God once more, God again praises the behavior of Job, who has remained blameless and upright and maintained his integrity. But this time the Adversary suggests that if he were allowed to hurt Job physically, Job would surely blaspheme God. Confident of Job's loyalty, God again takes the bet and puts Job in the Adversary's power, provided that Job's life is spared. Immediately the Adversary gives Job a severe inflammation from head to foot. Job takes a potsherd to scratch himself, while his wife urges him to blaspheme God and die. Job scolds her by saying that if they accept the good from God, they should also accept the bad. Once again, Job remains sinless.

At this point, it might appear that this is a story about how much torture Job can endure and still remain loyal to God, but that would make for a grisly and not very informative tale. Later it will become clear that this question of enduring suffering as opposed to blaspheming is actually an auxiliary theme. More on that later.

In any case, three of Job's friends come to see him in his misery and attempt to console and comfort him. They find Job so distorted by pain that he is unrecognizable. His friends tear their clothes, weep, throw dust onto his head, and sit silently with Job for seven days, in apparent empathy with him.

Job: Chapter 3

Finally, Job begins to speak. He curses the day he was born and the night he was conceived. He asks that the day of his birth be darkened, uncounted, and damned for not blocking his mother's womb. He asks why he didn't die at birth, because, if he had, he would now be at rest. He asks why he wasn't buried at birth like a stillborn, because, if he had been, he'd be free. He asks why God gives life and spirit to those who wait for death. What he dreaded has overtaken him, and he has no rest.

Job: Chapter 4

Eliphaz, one of Job's apparently empathic friends, answers him. After gentle and diplomatic opening remarks, Eliphaz quickly gets to the point, which is that, by suffering and not blaspheming, Job has set an inspiring example for others but that Job has now become unnerved. Eliphaz then encourages Job to have hope because, according to Eliphaz's theology, no innocent man has ever perished; only evil-doers are destroyed.

Eliphaz then says that he had a vision in which he heard a voice saying, "Can mortals be acquitted by God?" The idea is that, if God cannot trust even his angels, then God can trust mortals even less. Thus God cannot trust Job sufficiently to acquit him. Eliphaz gives a rationale for the theology of retribution, according to which God has no choice but to punish sinners; God cannot take the risk of acquitting such untrustworthy creatures as mortals and hence must punish them. Thus, simply by virtue of being mortal, Job is doomed to punishment. Of course, Eliphaz is assuming—incorrectly—that Job has sinned.

Job: Chapter 5

Eliphaz then implies that Job would be a fool to deny that he has done some mischief that would explain his situation. Job should appeal directly to God, because God offers hope for the wretched.

Moreover, Eliphaz says, Job should be happy that God is reproving him. If Job will only accept his suffering as divinely imposed discipline, then he will be redeemed from death and will be well again. Clearly, Eliphaz is assuming that Job has sinned and that God will conform to the following pattern: man sins, God punishes, man repents, and God forgives. Hence Eliphaz is urging Job to repent and be forgiven.

Job: Chapter 6

Job replies by saying that his anguish is so great that it has caused him to speak recklessly, but he still wants God to crush him—that is, to let him die, because he has exhausted all his resources for enduring. Job goes on to criticize his friends for being fickle, because, at the sight of misfortune, they take fright. Job says that all he wants from his friends is that they teach him where he has gone wrong. He then rebukes them for reproving him and not recognizing that he is in the right.

Job: Chapter 7

Ignoring his friends and speaking now to God, Job laments his distress. He cannot rest; his flesh is covered with maggots. His days go by without hope; he will go down to Sheol (hell, pictured as a garbage dump), and God will see him no more.

But Job pledges to continue complaining bitterly to God, because God has set a watch over him, as if Job were some monster that needed to be kept under surveillance. Job is sick of being supervised and of being frightened by dreams and visions. He asks again to die.

Job then asks God what there is about man that God should inspect and examine him at every moment. Why, Job asks, can't God look away from him for a while? And, if God is aware of some transgression of which Job is ignorant, why does God not pardon that transgression?

Job: Chapter 8

Bildad, another so-called friend, replies to Job by calling Job's statements arrogant and foolish and by reasserting the principle that God does not pervert justice. If Job's sons were killed, then, in Bildad's view, they were being punished for their transgressions. Bildad argues that, if Job is actually blameless and upright, God will protect him and grant him well-being. If Job will only look at history, according to Bildad, he will see that only those who forget God wither and that God does not despise the blameless or support evildoers.

As was said above, the theme of Job's suffering, over against his determination not to blaspheme God, is not the main theme of this story but rather an auxiliary theme. At this point, it becomes clear that the main theme around which the action takes place is whether or not God is constrained by the principle of punishing evildoers and rewarding those who do good or, as the text puts it, filling the mouths of the blameless with laughter. Job's friends are convinced that God always follows this principle, while Job knows from his own bitter experience that God is apparently not constrained by it. Meanwhile, Job's suffering provides the reason for this debate—a debate sometimes between Job and his friends and at other times between Job and God—to occur at all. And the theme of Job's not blaspheming maintains the tension between the two or three sides in the debate, because, if Job ever blasphemed, he would no longer be blameless.

Job: Chapter 9

Job ignores Bildad and speaks in a way that recalls his appeal to God in chapter 7. He says that he would like to have his day in court with God but that no man can win a suit against God. Who, Job asks rhetorically, can question this God who shakes the earth, spreads out the heavens, and performs great and unfathomable deeds? How could Job answer him or choose arguments against him? Even if Job were right, he says, he could not speak out. Even if Job could have a trial in court, who would summon God? And Job could never prove his case anyway, he says, because God destroys the blameless along with the guilty—a fact that clearly contradicts the theology of retribution.

Again Job laments his sorry state. His days fly by without happiness; he remains in dread of all his suffering. If only God would relieve his suffering and not let terror frighten him, he would speak out without fear, because he knows he is not in the wrong.

Given that Job's last two replies to his friends are not replies at all but appeals for divine intervention, Job is clearly starting to believe that the disagreement he has with his friends cannot be resolved through discussion with them and that a divine arbiter is required.

Job: Chapter 10

Disgusted with life, Job asks God not to condemn him but instead to tell him what the charge is against him. Job asks, with bitterness and pain, if God enjoys hurting good people and smiling upon the wicked. Obviously, this statement not only asserts that God is not acting according to the theology of retribution but also challenges God to explain the principle by which God is acting. In any case, Job then directly asserts his innocence and reminds God that only God can deliver him.

In this direct appeal to God, Job acknowledges that it is God who made him and shaped him. But then he asks if God has gone to that trouble only for the purpose of watching him sin and then not absolving him of his iniquity. Job boldly declares that God has nothing to be proud of in hunting Job as if he were an animal to be preyed upon. Why did God let him be born? And why, Job asks, can't God leave him alone for a while before Job goes into the land of darkness—that is, dies?

Significantly, Job's reluctance to argue with his friends, whose understanding of God and of Job's situation is far from what Job knows to be true, indicates that Job's real argument is with God. If the theology espoused by the friends were in any way the solution to Job's problems, then he would be trying to learn from them or negotiate with them. But since these friends are so completely wrongheaded, they serve only to annoy him and make him appeal to God instead. At the same time, of course, the fact that the theology of the friends is not at all helpful in Job's situation constitutes a resounding rebuttal of that theology.

Job: Chapter 11

Zophar, a third friend, accuses Job of being intentionally loquacious in order to conceal his guilt behind a flood of words. That approach might work with men, Zophar says, but, if God spoke, God would reveal Job's lack of wisdom.

Then Zophar talks about how powerful and all-knowing God is and asserts that no mere man could have such understanding. But if Job would only direct his mind to God and repent, Zophar asserts, he could hold his head high, and his life would be brighter than noon; he would lie down undisturbed, and the great would court his favor.

Job: Chapter 12

Not surprisingly, Job is extremely annoyed with Zophar's statement and declares that it is flippant, showing only contempt for his horrible suffering. Zophar fails to recognize, Job says, that robbers live untroubled in their tents and that those who provoke God are secure. In light of such realities, Zophar, who pretends to be so insightful about God and man, should, Job suggests, acknowledge that the theology of retribution is mistaken.

Job then advises Zophar to take a look at nature and discover that wisdom, courage, counsel, and understanding belong to God but that God also causes bad things to happen. For example, Job says, God causes judges to go mad, deprives trusted men of speech, pours disgrace upon great men, exalts nations and then destroys them, and makes the leaders of the people wander as if drunk in a trackless waste.

These examples all serve to demonstrate that the theology of retribution misrepresents God.

Job: Chapter 13

Job then asserts that he is as knowledgeable as Zophar, as if to say that Zophar is not helping at all. Thus Job prefers to argue directly with God. Zophar and his other two friends, Job says, are quacks and should keep silent rather than speak deceitfully for God. Job is convinced that God will reprove Zophar and find Zophar's statements to be empty platitudes.

At this point, it certainly seems that the aim of the book of Job is to show that the theology of retribution is indeed an empty platitude, but a platitude deeply engrained in the mind of the Jerusalem hardliners, who attempt to impose it on all Jews. This theology must be discredited—not once or twice—but repeatedly and authoritatively. It's a theology that dies hard and, every time it's killed, seems to come back to life in people's minds. That is why this argument between Job and his friends has gone on so long and will continue even longer. Clearly, only God can settle this argument.

In any case, Job is determined to run the risk of making his case before God, and he is sure that, if he is granted that privilege, his being allowed to come before God in and of itself will be the proof of his innocence, because no impious man can come into God's presence.

Speaking to God, Job says that he has a very good case but that, before God summons him to respond, God must stop terrorizing him and making him suffer. Job asks why God hides his face and treats Job like an enemy, especially since Job is as weak as a driven leaf or a piece of straw.

It should be noted that Job's insistence on having his case heard before God reflects several distinct but related desires on Job's part: first, to see his friends' theology authoritatively disproved, then, to be found innocent himself, and, finally, to understand God and the way God operates. Everything in the narrative thus far foreshadows the satisfaction of the first two of these desires. After all, the narrative would achieve nothing by leaving the outcome of this debate unresolved, and Job's innocence has been a given from the outset. But the possibility of Job's coming to understand God and God's operations remains far from certain.

Job: Chapter 14

Job then reflects on what it's like to be a human being. A human being, he says to God, has a short and precarious life that is limited by God in many ways. When a tree dies, it grows back, but not so with a man; he lies down never to rise until the end of time. Thus God destroys man's hope and humbles him. And just in case Job's suffering is a result of divine wrath, Job asks if God would hide Job until God's anger passes.

Job's reflection on the human condition takes the form of an appeal for a speedy trial before God or, failing that, for a delay until God is in a better mood.

Job: Chapter 15

Eliphaz, who has not spoken since chapters 4 and 5, re-enters the discussion in a particularly aggravating way. He reiterates Bildad's accusation that Job is hiding behind empty words and is thus subverting piety. He also scolds Job for acting like the sole possessor of wisdom and for venting his anger on God. How can God be expected to find Job innocent, Eliphaz says, when not even the heavens are guiltless in God's sight?

Eliphaz then repeats some traditional wisdom based on the theology of retribution—namely, that God punishes the robber and the ruthless, who will never be rich but will instead lose every good thing they have.

The irony is that Eliphaz and the other two friends are the ones who use empty words—and for no better purpose than tediously to reiterate the theology of retribution, despite the fact that Job has already amply demonstrated that theology's lack of explanatory power.

Job: Chapters 16 and 17

Job remarks wryly that he often hears such things that Eliphaz utters. Then Job mocks Eliphaz for daring to barrage him with words, in ignorance of Job's real situation. If their places were reversed, Job says, he would barrage Eliphaz with words, for all the good it would do, the implication being that Eliphaz is too thick-headed to be worth arguing with. Job defends his appeals to God by saying that he has nothing to lose by speaking out to God. For this reason, Job now directs his speech to God and says that God has worn him out, destroyed his community, shriveled him, torn him, and persecuted him, so that Job's friends revile him and inflame themselves against him. God has set Job up as his target, Job says, despite Job's innocence. As a result, only God can testify for him, he says, and may this testimony come soon, because Job is ready for the graveyard. Job calls on God to speak up for him against these mocking men, that is, his friends, who have no understanding or wisdom.

These repeated examples of the friends' stubborn wrongheadedness and of Job's exhaustion and frustration provide a rather good picture of how deeply entrenched the theology of retribution was among the hardlines of the Jerusalem elite, of how stubbornly it was defended in spite of all the evidence to the contrary, and of how much effort was required to uproot it.

Job: Chapter 18

Bildad replies, accusing Job of calling his friends idiots, as if Job thought that the whole world order would change for Job's sake. Significantly, Bildad considers the whole world order to be contained and reflected in the theology of retribution.

Bildad then reiterates the platitudes associated with his theology: the light of the wicked fails; his strides are hobbled; his schemes overthrow him; the noose tightens on him; terrors assault him; his family suffers disaster; he has no name abroad; he has no descendants. Such is the fate, he says, of him who knew not God.

Job: Chapter 19

Job says in reply that his friends may continue to abuse him, but they should also know that God has wronged him and that Job has cried out for justice but gotten none. God has broken Job down and blocked him at every turn; God has made him repulsive to his servants, family, and friends. His friends should rather pity him, Job says, because God has struck him. Why, he asks, are his friends pursuing him as if they were God? Yet Job is sure that God will vindicate him while he is still alive and that his friends will be judged.

As Job's frustration with his friends has grown in intensity, so have his cries for God to intervene and judge him.

Job: Chapter 20

Zophar replies, claiming to feel insulted, primarily because Job has been rejecting what Zophar believes to be the organizing principle of the universe—namely, the theology of retribution. Zophar then recites a whole litany of platitudes about how God punishes the wicked.

Thus, Job's friends, by endlessly repeating their platitudes, not only fail to take Job seriously but also reveal the intellectual poverty of their theology. They amply display their self-righteousness, insensitivity, and ignorance. These friends, one should recall, represent the hardliners of the Jerusalem elite.

Job: Chapter 21

Job replies, telling his so-called friends that his complaint is not with them but with God. He also says that of course he loses his patience, because the wicked—unlike Job—live on, prosper, and grow wealthy; their children stay with them, and their homes are secure. God does not punish them. They spend their days in happiness and die in peace. They spurn God and reject God's ways, yet seldom does calamity befall them. But no man can instruct God and thus change God's mind, and for that reason, Job says, the impious rich man dies untroubled, while the pious poor man is left to die embittered. Thus, Job concludes, the so-called consolation the friends have offered him is empty and full of perfidy. Which is to say that the theology of retribution is a total fraud.

Job: Chapter 22

Eliphaz challenges Job by asking, rhetorically, if Job thinks God is punishing him for being blameless. Does Job not recognize, says Eliphaz, that he has sinned, by abusing the weak, and that his current situation results directly from that sin?

Eliphaz asks if Job has observed the path trodden by evil men. If he did, says Eliphaz, he would see the evil consumed by fire and the innocent laugh with scorn. Hence Job should stay close to God, and good things will come to him. He should seek God's favor, and his wishes will be fulfilled.

This is another example of the friends' blindly—or perhaps not so blindly—ignoring the facts of Job's situation, in a stubborn attempt to defend the theology of retribution. When such attempts first occurred in the story, they seemed to reflect a certain pious naiveté, but as they have continued relentlessly in the face of indisputable evidence to the contrary, they have come to look rather abusive. The intent of this story is thus to demonstrate that the theology of retribution is mistaken—not merely in some harmlessly empty-headed and naïve manner—but in a hurtful and mean-spirited way. If this story is aimed at the Jerusalem hardliners, the implication is that they are not only promoting a mistaken theology but doing so knowingly and with bad intentions.

Job: Chapters 23 and 24

Job laments his inability to reach God. If he could only set his case before God, God would respond and not accuse him.

No matter where Job looks, though, God is hidden. If God assayed him, he says, God would find him pure as gold. But since

God remains hidden, Job says, he is terrified by God's invisible presence. Yet he does not feel cut off from God.

Why, Job asks, doesn't God reserve special times for judgment? God's actions are unpredictable, Job says. People commit all sorts of sins: removing boundary stones, rustling cattle, chasing the needy off the roads, forcing the poor into hiding, seizing a child as a pledge. The oppressed cry out, but God doesn't seem to care.

People commit evil deeds and think these go unseen. Job prays that such people be cursed, eaten by worms, forgotten, and broken. God protects evil-doers for a while, but, Job implores God, let them wither and die.

In this speech, Job seeks not only to be judged by God and found innocent but also to have God judge evil-doers and condemn them. Job already knows perfectly well that God does not feel constrained by the principle of punishing the evil and rewarding the good, but, Job insists, God should nevertheless punish the wicked.

Job: Chapter 25

Bildad responds to Job's plea for judgment by saying that, if even the stars are not pure enough for God, no man can be cleared of guilt, especially since man is little better than a worm or maggot. This is the same argument that Eliphaz made in chapter 4—that is, "Can mortals be acquitted by God?"

This particular argument takes the theology of retribution to an even more abusive level, by claiming that in the final analysis there is no such thing as forgiveness: a sinner is permanently condemned.

Job: Chapter 26

Job denounces Bildad as too stupid and too lacking in wisdom and authority to make such a statement. Only God, who performed mighty deeds in creation, is qualified to judge Job.

Job: Chapter 27

It is God, Job says, who has deprived him of justice and embittered his life. But Job vows never to speak wrong or utter deceit. He will maintain his integrity and persist in his righteousness as long as he lives.

Job then expresses his desire that the wicked not receive God's favor but rather lose their families, go hungry, be buried in a plague with no one to mourn them, lose all their money, and be carried far away by the wind; and that the innocent get the evildoers' share of silver.

Such is the justice that Job asks God to perform. It should be noted that this appeal is based not on the theology of retribution but simply on God's prerogative to do as God chooses.

Job: Chapter 28

Job explains that man explores but that God sets limits. Where, then, can wisdom be found? Job is convinced that it cannot be found in the land of the living. Yet nothing, he says, is more precious than wisdom.

But where does it come from? It is hidden from the eyes of all the living, Job says. Only God can see where it comes from; God measured it and probed it. At this point, Job discovers what wisdom really is: "Fear of the Lord is wisdom: to shun evil is understanding."

It should be noted that fear of the Lord—that is, awesome respect for God—implies that God operates differently from man and in ways that defy human understanding, and thus that the theology of retribution, which pretends to enable predictions of God's every action, represents a lack of wisdom.

Job: Chapter 29

Job longs for the days when God graced his life with children, pleasure, and respect from the elders. At that time, Job saved the widow, the poor, and the lost. Justice was his turban and cloak. He helped the blind, the lame, and the needy. He defended the stranger and chastised the wrong-doer. Job had thought that those days would go on and on, those days when the people around him honored him and depended upon him, and he lived like a king among his troops.

Job: Chapter 30

But all that has changed, he says. Younger men deride him, while the men he used to know are either old and shouted at as if they were thieves, or are dead. And Job has become the butt of scoundrels' jokes. They abhor him and spit in his face, because God has humbled him. His dignity has vanished, and he is physically vanishing as well; his waist is no bigger than his neck.

The younger men of whom Job speaks are his so-called friends. They have been, figuratively speaking, spitting in his face. The implication is that the Jerusalem hardliners are young scoundrels.

Job cries out again to God, but God does not answer. God, he laments, has become cruel and is harassing him. Why is this happening to him? he wants to know. Didn't he weep for the unfortunate? Didn't he grieve for the needy? Days of misery now confront him; his skin is black and peeling; his bones are charred; he has become as feral as jackals and ostriches. There is nothing left for him, he sighs, but mourning and weeping.

Job: Chapter 31

Job wonders what fate God has decreed for him. Surely, he says, calamity and misfortune are for evil-doers. Surely God is observing him and knows that he has not done evil, has not committed adultery, and has never brushed aside a servant's complaint. There follows a series of rhetorical questions: Did Job ever deny the needs of a widow, of an orphan, or of the poor? If he ever did, he says, let his arm fall off and his elbow break. Did he ever trust in gold or rejoice in great wealth? Did he ever rejoice in his enemy's misfortune? No sojourner spent the night in the open, because Job opened his doors to him. Did Job ever hide his sins as Adam did?

If only he had someone to give him a hearing. If only God would meet him in court, he would give God an account like the one a good soldier would give to his commanding officer, and God would see that Job has never taken what was not rightfully his.

Then having made his case, Job falls silent.

Job: Chapter 32

Job's three friends stop replying to him because they see that he thinks he's right. But now Elihu, a younger man who has been silently observing the scene, decides to speak. He is angry with Job for thinking himself righteous before God and is angry with the three friends, too, because they have found no reply to Job and have merely condemned him.

Elihu says that, because he is so young, he has waited until now to speak, but that wisdom has nothing to do with years and everything to do with whether God has given a man understanding. Elihu is concerned over the fact that the three friends have given up trying to convince Job and have decided to let God do it. So, then, Elihu is going to try to convince Job, but not, he claims, with the same arguments that the three friends used. Elihu says that he is bursting with words eager to come out and that he will not hold back.

Job: Chapter 33

Elihu calls upon Job to answer and emphasizes that, though formed by the spirit of God, he (Elihu) is a human being, made of clay just like Job, and should thus not be intimidating for Job. As evidence that Job is not intimidated, says Elihu, Job has already stated in Elihu's hearing that he is guiltless and considers God his enemy.

In this, Elihu asserts, Job is wrong, because God is greater than any man and does not reply to man directly but rather through dreams and visions that open man's understanding and discipline him to turn away from evil actions. It may happen that a man suffers horribly and is on the verge of death, but if someone is there to declare the man's righteousness, God has mercy on him, saves him from the pit, and makes him young again. Then the redeemed man declares publically that he sinned but was not paid back for it. Elihu affirms that God does these things and hence that Job should pay attention and listen to Elihu.

This is a strange argument in that it appears to offer a way to circumvent the theology of retribution. Elihu seems to be suggesting that he might be willing to declare Job's innocence before God, so that Job would not be paid back for his sin. For all practical purposes, this suggestion puts Elihu in the place of God. Thus it is predictable that, if God ever does hear Job's case, Elihu will have to answer to God for his hubris, in much the same way as the three friends are already in trouble for pretending to have God all figured out and under control.

Job: Chapter 34

Elihu calls upon those present to decide for themselves about Job's claim of innocence. Elihu then rebukes Job for denying the validity of the theology of retribution, since Job has argued that man does not necessarily gain anything by being in God's favor.

Elihu affirms that God does not act wickedly or pervert justice but instead repays a man according to his actions. In saying that, Elihu contradicts what he has just said in chapter 33. In any case, if Job admits that God governs the world, Elihu argues, how can Job claim that the one who governs hates justice? God is an impartial judge, so that if a great man does wrong, God removes him. God sees every human act, so that the evil-doer has no place to hide. If they are disloyal to God, God strikes down the mighty, along with the wicked. God also hears the cry of the poor and the needy. But Job's case is different, according to Elihu, because Job does not admit his iniquity and ask for pardon. Thus Job lacks understanding and increases his sin by multiplying his statements against God.

It seems clear in this chapter that Elihu does little more than revert to the standard arguments based on the theology of retribution.

Job: Chapter 35

Elihu criticizes Job for saying that his argument is really with God and not with other people. The basis for that criticism, Elihu argues, is that both one's wickedness and one's righteousness affect only other people, not God.

Clearly, Elihu's argument is flawed in several ways: first, the Hebrew Bible offers ample textual evidence that God cares deeply about human behavior, and second, Elihu's argument does nothing either to support or to undercut the theology of retribution, which is the real issue.

Elihu contends that the oppressed shout out against the power of the great but do not cry out to God, because they know that God gives the oppressed strength, knowledge, and wisdom. When the oppressed finally do cry out, God hears them but does not respond, Elihu claims, because of the arrogance of evil men. Eventually, after a long wait, God finally deals with their case. The implication is that Job should be waiting patiently for God rather than demanding his day in court.

This is another rather confused and presumptuous argument. Elihu is once again making the mistake of pretending to speak for God, as if Elihu knew that God doesn't respond to the oppressed and that the reason for God's reluctance had something to do with the arrogance of evil men. In short, Elihu is attempting to manage and control God in much the same way as do the three friends.

In a clumsy attempt to defend God, Elihu, like the three friends, has been making a fool of himself and at the same time disrespecting God.

Job: Chapter 36

Elihu claims to have more to say, but all he does is recite another litany of platitudes based on the theology of retribution, to which God is supposedly so faithful that men should glorify God's conduct.

Earlier it was noted that the three friends often sound rather nasty in the way they ruthlessly attempt to impose a theology that simply doesn't fit, but Elihu, by contrast, sounds merely stupid and naïve.

Presumably, Elihu represents another unpleasant characteristic of the ruling elite.

Job: Chapter 37

Elihu says that God is powerful and works wonders that man cannot understand. God controls the weather, as well as other events, and makes them accomplish his commands, either as scourges or as blessings. Elihu urges Job to consider the marvels of God and to realize that man, who dwells in darkness, cannot argue with God. Job would do better, according to Elihu, to reflect on God's awesome power, justice, and righteousness.

This statement contains elements of truth but is nevertheless flawed. God is indeed awesome in power, justice, and righteousness, but Elihu, while presuming to have insight into God's purposes and actions, actually has a distorted understanding of the way God works. God's justice and righteousness do not conform to the pattern proposed by the theology of retribution. A further problem with this speech is that Job does not dwell in darkness—that is, he is not confused; he is perfectly lucid. In short, Elihu presumes to advocate for God, and that act would be highly problematic even if Elihu were correct in what he said.

Job: Chapter 38

Having sat silently through thirty-four long chapters of unrelentingly annoying dialogue, God finally replies to Job out of the tempest—an important image because it emphasizes the immense difference between God and man.

In what one must assume is a thunderous voice, God asks who it is who has been speaking without knowledge. This is an ambiguous question because, though apparently directed at Job, it could refer just as well to Elihu and the three friends. In any event, God commands Job to gird his loins—that is, prepare for a fight. Job's day in court will be rough.

What follows is a long and beautiful series of rhetorical questions designed to make it perfectly clear that God alone is responsible for creation and all its wonders and that God alone understands such things. These questions have the effect of underscoring the infinite difference between man and God and of dressing down anyone who presumes to speak for God or who challenges God's authority. Once again there is ambiguity, because God could be addressing not only Job but also his so-called friends.

Job: Chapter 39

God continues to ask rhetorical questions. This time they all have to do with the mysteries surrounding animals: for example, why they give birth when they do, why they occupy a certain habitat, why their bodies are the way they are, why they behave as they do. Just as in the preceding chapter, the purpose of these questions is to remind Job and his friends that their knowledge is very limited and that true understanding belongs to God alone.

Job: Chapter 40

God says that it is now time for Job, who is getting his day in court, to respond. Job does respond but very meekly, saying, "See, I am of small worth; what can I answer you?" Job then promises to say no more.

Then God speaks to Job again out of the tempest and invites him to get ready for something like a boxing match. God will punch Job with a question, and Job will have to punch back with an answer.

The first questions are: "Would you impugn my justice? Would you condemn me that you may be right? Have you an arm like God's?" God explains what these questions mean by urging Job to clothe himself in glory and majesty and then see if he could humble every proud man. If Job could do that, God would praise him.

The purpose of these questions is not merely to scold Job for insisting on being right even at God's expense, but also and especially to teach Job that only God can resolve the debate Job has been having with his four friends and that it is not Job's place to attempt to humble his friends; that's God's business. This is a surprisingly comforting statement for Job, because it tells him that he was quite right to demand his day in court and that—no matter how hard God has already been on him or how hard God may punch him in this sparring match—God is on Job's side.

The next question involves behemoth, the awful sea monster that was the first animal God created. Could Job grab it by its eyes, pierce its nose with hooks, press down its tongue with a rope, or pierce its jaw with a barb? Could Job get behemoth to speak softly to him and become his slave?

The point of these questions is that Job needs to be able to distinguish between what belongs to God and what belongs to Job, between God's business and Job's business. Once again, this is an encouraging message for Job, because it implies that God intends to make rebuttal of the theology of retribution God's business.

Job: Chapter 41

God now explains another aspect of the behemoth imagery: just as Job could not stand up to behemoth, neither can he stand up to God. And just as behemoth is king over all proud beasts, so will God humble proud men who dare put themselves in the place of God. Here, just as earlier, God's statements apply as much to the friends as to Job, so that Job, like the reader, is waiting to see exactly what God intends to do.

Job: Chapter 42

Although Job promised in chapter 40 that he would speak no more, he speaks again anyway, saying that he knows that God can do everything and that nothing is impossible for God. This statement is not only a sign of humility before God and loyalty to God; it should be understood as subtle encouragement for God to do what God's previous statements have implied—namely, to declare Job innocent and rebut the theology of retribution.

Job now refers to the ambiguity inherent in God's statements by asking seriously the same question that God asked rhetorically when God first intervened in the debate back in chapter 38: "Who is this who obscures counsel without knowledge?" In other words, is it Job's friends or is it Job? Job's question is rather aggressive because it calls upon God to stop stalling with long stories about behemoths and to take action. But why shouldn't Job ask an aggressive question? After all, didn't God say that this conversation would be a real boxing match? So Job took the risk and responded to God with a tough question. But since God has been emphasizing the immeasurable difference between man and God, Job humbly backs away from his question by saying that he spoke without understanding and that only now, in this intimate meeting with God, does he finally see and thus want to recant and repent.

"Recant" and "repent" might seem like an admission of guilt or failure, but the reality is that Job has achieved a great victory, because he has succeeded in pushing into action this God who for many long chapters sat idly by and let Job do battle alone against his disloyal friends. The reality also is that Job did not speak without understanding; he was right all along. The only part Job didn't understand was how difficult it would be and how long it would take to get God to intervene on his side. Thus, Job's humility at the end is really a discreet celebration: God is finally going to vindicate Job and disprove his friends' wrongheaded theology.

Having been spurred into action by Job, God speaks to Eliphaz and says that he is incensed at him and his friends for not telling the truth about God the way Job did. God instructs them to go to Job and make an offering. Then God shows favor to Job and restores his fortunes two-fold. All his family and true friends have a festive meal with him in his house. God blesses the latter years of Job's life with vast herds of cattle and with seven sons and three exceptionally beautiful daughters. So Job has a long life and dies contented.

The Depiction of God in the Book of Job

Since the book of Job is clearly a debate about the nature and conduct of God and since this debate ends up being judged by the only person capable of judging it—namely, God—it certainly seems appropriate to reflect on the way God is depicted in this book.

In chapter 1 of the book of Job, God makes two bets with the Adversary. In the first bet, God permits the Adversary to take away all the blessings that God has given to Job—children and possessions—because God has great confidence in Job's loyalty. In other words, God is sure that Job understands that their relationship does not depend on Job's having all those blessings. Hence God can withdraw those blessings in perfect confidence that Job will remain loyal to God and not blaspheme. In thus acting, God is rejecting the theology of retribution. If God were acting according to the theology of retribution, God would feel constrained by the principle of always rewarding those who are blameless, and, since Job is unquestionably blameless, God would not be able to take the Adversary's bet. When God withdraws Job's blessings, God is acting freely and without constraint and is thus rejecting the theology of retribution.

God wins the first bet, and so the Adversary makes an even more challenging offer. He says that, if God will let him hurt Job physically, then Job will surely blaspheme. God takes this bet, too, because of his immense confidence in Job.

It might seem that God, in making these bets, is being rather reckless with Job's welfare, and these are, in fact, rather risky bets. But the implication is that Job and God have a solid relationship that can survive the horrors that Job endures. It is also implied that the theology of retribution has such committed and stubborn supporters that God must employ an extreme test in order to debunk it.

The physical pain Job endures is bad enough, but far worse is the psychological torture that he suffers at the hands of four so-called friends, who ruthlessly and relentlessly pummel him with platitudes in order to convince him that he is only getting the punishment he deserves for having somehow sinned. Throughout this seemingly interminable verbal battering of which Job is the victim, God says nothing. God might seem less than sympathetic by remaining silent for so long, but the length of that silence and the cruelty of the so-called friends suggest just how protracted and harsh the struggle against the theology of retribution has been in Judah. In any case, God's prolonged silence gives the so-called friends the opportunity they need to air every conceivable argument in favor of the theology of retribution. In this way, when God finally intervenes and authoritatively debunks this theology, every pro-retribution argument has already been used and been found wanting. Thus there can be no rebuttal to God's debunking of the friends' theology.

The anticipation of God's finally speaking is more keenly felt because of Job's repeated, anguished calls for God to give him his day in court and declare him innocent. These calls for justice have the effect of provoking the four friends to greater efforts to convict him, especially since they believe that Job must have sinned and thus that his calls for justice are an insult to God, in addition to whatever sin they think he must have committed.

Importantly, the sheer brutality of the debate is also meant to show that this question of what one believes about God's character and behavior is no trivial concern. If God were as pictured by the theology of retribution, God would, for all practical purposes, be under human control and thus would be greatly diminished in comparison with God's true nature. If God were as imagined by the theology of retribution, God would be reduced to a political tool or puppet designed to lend authority to human decisions. For example, the victors in any contest, regardless of what means they had used to win, could claim to have God's blessing; the rich, no matter what means they used to gain their wealth, could claim to possess no more than what God thought they deserved. In other words, God became an instrument of propaganda for justifying all sorts of social inequities.

When God finally intervenes in the debate, God immediately launches into a three-chapter-long speech on the incomparable majesty, power, and greatness of God. The purpose of this speech is, obviously, to combat and reject the theology of retribution, which, if not thus refuted, would indeed have the effect of diminishing God. In other words, God intervenes not only for the sake of Job but also in self-defense.

Significantly, although the so-called friends have repeatedly accused Job of sinning, they are the ones who have sinned by misrepresenting God, whereas Job has remained upright and blameless. If the theology of retribution were valid, God would be obliged to punish the friends, but God opts not to do that. Instead, God simply tells them that they have not spoken the truth. Acting graciously, God tells them that God will not treat them vilely. In this way, both God's long speech and God's treatment of the so-called friends indicate that God is a supremely gracious God and does not operate according to the theology of retribution.

Similarly, God is not in any sense obliged to restore Job's fortunes; all Job ever asked for was to be heard and found innocent. But God freely chooses not only to restore Job's fortunes but to give him twice what he had before. Thus the story ends in a grand finale of grace.

The purpose of the book of Job is to make sure that, as the Jews develop an identity based not merely on their residence in Judah but on their loyalty to the one true God, they correctly come to understand this God. If the Jews cannot be disabused of the theology of retribution, their conception of God remains false and thus vitiates their role as the people of God.

In conclusion, the book of Job points to a battle that was waging among the intellectual leaders of postexilic Judah over the right to define and determine the content and character of the new monotheism that was developing after the exile. The hardliners argued for a God they could predict and control, whereas the dissenter who wrote the book of Job argued for a gracious God not subject to any human limits or constraints.

Rahab

Preliminary Remarks

The relevance of the story of Rahab (Joshua 2) is that it shows God working through a foreigner—and, what's more, a woman—and thus reveals that God is radically inclusive and seeks to embrace all humankind. Although the action of the story takes place on the eve of the Israelite invasion of Canaan, this story does not come from that early period but rather dates from postexilic Judah. The reason for this postexilic dating is not only that, historically speaking, the Israelites never invaded Canaan, but also that postexilic Judah was a period in which women and foreigners for the first time became a politically important issue. Thus, a story about a foreign woman like Rahab would have been timely and relevant in the postexilic period, but not in any previous period.

The story of Rahab

Joshua, the commander of the Israelites, told his soldiers that their wives and children will remain on the east side of the Jordan while they, his fighting men, cross the river and take possession of the land of Canaan, which the Lord, the God of Israel, has assigned to them. But before such an invasion, Joshua secretly sends two spies to reconnoiter the city of Jericho.

The spies set out and come to the house of a harlot named Rahab. It is important to realize that Rahab is an excellent choice for a story about a foreigner because she is an extreme example of a foreigner. She is not some highly educated and respectable citizen whom one could imagine fitting in with the Jerusalem elite; she is a harlot. Her social status is very low, both because of her profession and because she is a woman alone in the world, without the protection of a man. Nothing at all is socially positive about her status. She is in every respect a counterintuitive choice as protagonist. The reason for making such a person the protagonist is that, if something good can happen with or through such an apparently debased foreign woman, the Jerusalem hardliners' policy of banning foreign wives will be discredited and rebutted. The aim of this story is precisely to shame the Jerusalem hardliners for their xenophobia and misogyny.

Returning to the story, when the two spies come to Rahab's house, she gives them lodging. Immediately, the king of Jericho hears that spies have entered his territory, and he orders Rahab to turn these men over to him. But by then Rahab has hidden the two spies and responds to the king's orders with the following half-truth: "It is true, the men did come to me, but I didn't know where they were from. And at dark, when the gate was about to be closed, the men left; and I don't know where the men went. Quick, go after them, for you can overtake them."

Rahab's lie is both bold and clever. What's bold about it is that she is lying straight-faced—not to someone on the street—but to the king himself and on a matter of the gravest importance. What's clever about her lie is that it contains enough truth to be believable, and at the same time it sends the king's henchmen off in the wrong direction, a ploy that gives Rahab time to figure out what to do next. Rahab is clearly a woman who is willing to take great risks and is capable of thinking on her feet. But the most striking feature of this episode is that, on a moment's notice and without any previous knowledge of these spies, this foreign woman gives them lodging and lies for them. There is no practical, plausible explanation for her action. Like the character Rahab herself, her action is counterintuitive. No one would ever expect a foreigner, let alone a harlot, to act so audaciously, and, in the biblical literature, such counterintuitive behavior is a sure sign of God's involvement.

Rahab

The king's henchmen depart the city, and the city gates are shut and locked behind them. The spies remain hidden on the roof under stalks of flax, but, before the spies fall asleep, Rahab goes up to the roof to talk with them and makes a statement that, like her other actions to this point, is absolutely astounding. In 2:9–13, she says:

> I know the Lord has given the country to you, because dread of you has fallen upon us, and all the inhabitants of the land are quaking before you. For we have heard how the Lord dried up the waters of the Sea of Reeds for you when you left Egypt, and what you did to Sihon and Og, the two Amorite kings across the river, whom you doomed. When we heard about it, we lost heart, and no man had any more spirit left because of you; for the Lord your God is the only God in heaven above and on earth below. Now, since I have shown loyalty to you, swear to me by the Lord that you in turn will show loyalty to my family. Provide me with a reliable sign that you will spare the lives of my father and mother, my brothers and sisters, and all who belong to them, and save us from death.

This speech leaves the spies dumbfounded. They have no way of knowing that Rahab has lied for their benefit and has seriously risked herself for them. All they know is that, for reasons unknown, this foreign harlot has hidden them under piles of flax on the roof. Without any introduction, she says that the Lord has given the country to them, and in this way she clearly indicates that she has been in communication with their God, the God of Israel. What an amazing confession from a foreigner—and even more amazing from a harlot. She even knows what the king of Jericho apparently does not know and what even, among the Israelites, only Moses and Joshua know—namely, that the Lord has assigned this land to the Israelites.

She tells the spies that the people of Jericho are in dread because they have heard about the exodus from Egypt and about the Israelites' victories against Sihon and Og. But the reader knows differently. The king of Jericho's aggressive action to apprehend the spies and protect his kingdom is surely not a sign of dread. The king has instead assumed a resolute posture of resistance; he is definitely not quaking. Hence Rahab's statement about popular dread appears to be more an attempt by her to build up Israelite morale than it is a factually accurate report. How wildly counterintuitive it is to receive such encouragement from a foreigner whose country is about to be invaded. More striking still is Rahab's confession that the God of Israel is the only God, especially since even Israelites in the period in which this event is set were not sure of that. Obviously, this text dates from after the Babylonian exile, when the Jews finally did become monotheists. In any event, Rahab's confession of loyalty to the one God is counterintuitive because no foreigner would conceivably have had such a thought unless it came from God.

Significantly, the Israelites themselves are not at all sure of their ability to take possession of the land that, according to Moses and Joshua, the Lord has assigned to them; otherwise Joshua would not have considered it necessary to send these two spies secretly to reconnoiter Jericho. These two spies are astonished that a foreign harlot is more confident of their eventual victory than they are. Moreover, she seems to understand better than they do the significance of the Lord's role in all this. In short, Rahab seems in every way more in touch with God than they are.

Rahab is in fact so confident that the Israelites will take possession of Jericho that she makes the spies promise that, when the invasion comes, they will spare the lives of her family. The spies accept the bargain and pledge themselves even to death. If she does not disclose their mission, they say, they will keep their pledge to her when the Lord gives them the land. Note that the spies now believe that the Lord will indeed give them the land; Rahab has convinced them.

Rahab now lowers the spies down by a rope through the window of her house, which is built into the city wall, and tells them to head for the hills, stay there for three days until the king's henchmen have returned to the city, and then go on their way. Clearly, Rahab is not only intrepid in action but also clever in planning.

But the spies, thinking about the bargain they have made with Rahab, tell her that they won't be able to guarantee her family's safety when the invasion comes, unless she ties a length of crimson cord to the window through which she is letting them down. Rahab must also gather all her family into her house, and they must remain inside during the battle. If they venture out and get killed, it won't be the Israelites' fault. The spies also remind Rahab not to disclose their mission, though this last reminder seems unnecessary since Rahab is obviously on their side.

Rahab lets them down and ties the cord on her window. The spies follow Rahab's instructions, and the king's henchmen return to the city empty-handed. The spies then report to Joshua exactly what Rahab told them, namely, that the Lord has delivered the whole land into their power and that the inhabitants of the land are quaking before the Israelites.

The point of the story of Rahab is that the Israelites owe their successful possession of the land to the divinely inspired intervention of a foreign harlot who in many ways is closer to God than they are. The significance of such an event is that the xenophobia of the intended audience, the Jerusalem elite—who want to exclude foreigners, especially women—is contrary to God's will and runs the risk of obstructing God's activity on behalf of the Jews. The story makes it clear that God does indeed communicate with foreigners and work through them and thus that some foreigners understand more about God than do the Jerusalem elite. Hence the policy of banishing foreign wives is a serious mistake that hurts the Jewish community.

In this way, this story is a protest against both xenophobia and misogyny, which the story implies would not only be stupid and wrongheaded, but actually damages the community that practices them. The story also demonstrates that if a community acts as do the two spies—rejecting xenophobia and misogyny—and remains open to foreigners and women, good things happen.

The Relevance of This Text for Post-Exilic Judah

At a time when the hardliners among the Jerusalem elite are banning foreign wives and blaming women for bringing polytheism into the

The Struggle to Define God

community of monotheists, the surprising protagonist of this story is both a foreigner and a harlot. For the hardliners in Jerusalem, she would be considered double trouble, to be avoided at all costs.

But how could even the most xenophobic leader in Jerusalem look down upon a foreigner whose knowledge of God exceeds that of these spies and even that of their commanders? Neither the spies nor their generals can claim to have the same intimacy that she has with God. Given the fact that the main faction of the Jerusalem elite think of themselves as the arbiters of this newly-emerged monotheism, an encounter with a foreigner who knows more than they do—even if she is only a literary character—must give them pause and make them re-think their policy on foreign women.

What sense would it make to ban a foreigner who is obviously acting in partnership with God? And if God enters into partnership even with harlots, how can the elite justify their misogyny? Does not their policy on foreign wives risk obstructing God's work in the world? Moreover, if God is actively reaching out to and working through foreigners, how can the Jerusalem elite justify limiting access to the community of monotheists?

Thus, this text urges the people in power to ask themselves whether they are helping or hindering their God.

Final reflections

The Fate of These Four Texts

AS THE FOREGOING DISCUSSION suggests, each of these four texts is, in its own way, an extraordinary literary achievement. In very few words, the book of Jonah subtly rebuts the theology of retribution and portrays God as gracious. By contrast, the book of Job takes a hard-hitting approach that finally exhausts both the reader and Job's friends' arguments and that requires God himself to intervene in order to refute the theology of retribution and proclaim the validity of the theology of grace. The story of Rahab, though very brief, effectively promotes inclusivism, open-mindedness, and gender equality, and so does the book of Ruth, which is also both touching and inspirational. In short, these four texts portray God as gracious and radically inclusive. But as the stubbornness of Jonah and of Job's friends and their resistance to the evidence indicate, it would be naïve to expect that the hardliners in Jerusalem saw the light and adopted the progressive thinking of these texts. In fact, what occurred in postexilic Judah is that the theology of retribution became dominant, while xenophobia and misogyny continued unabated.

The book of Job, in which four so-called friends gang up against the suffering Job and batter him relentlessly with arguments that disregard his real situation, seems to imply that the author of this text was fully aware of the stubbornness and strength of the hardliners and that he did not realistically expect his book to convert them. Much the same can be said for the other three texts studied. These authors made their protests in the knowledge

The Struggle to Define God

that their work would not have much immediate political effect, but they went ahead and protested nevertheless. These four texts are, in fact, small islands of progressive thinking in a vast sea of hardline biblical theology.

And, yet, enough Jews remained interested in and inspired by these four texts that, around 400 CE, when the Jews began deciding which religious texts would be considered sacred and thus included in the Hebrew Bible, these four liberal texts were included.

In order to get an idea of intellectual developments among Jews in the period between the first publication of these four texts and their later inclusion in the Hebrew Bible, it is helpful to consider what the Talmud says about God's justice and mercy. The Talmud compiles the oral reflections offered by great rabbis on the meaning of the written Torah. Since every law or instruction needs to be interpreted before it can be applied, the belief among Jews was that the Torah had, from its earliest origins, always existed in both oral and written form. Although the Talmud did not begin to assume written form until the third century CE, it includes rabbinical interpretations from much earlier periods.

In any case, the Talmud's views on God are surprisingly liberal. In fact, in the Talmud, the theology of the four texts studied in this book became orthodoxy. The rabbis follow Genesis 18:25 in thinking of God as the Judge of all the earth, who holds his creatures to account for their manner of living and who draws to himself the person whose acts are good.[1] But virtually every time the rabbis speak of God's justice, they associate it with God's compassion. They also find an interplay of justice and mercy throughout the Torah. The Hebrew Bible has two main appellations for God: ELOHIM and JHWH.[2] To the first of these, the Talmud assigns the aspect of judgment, and to the second the aspect of mercy. Thus, wherever these two appellations are found in the biblical text, the rabbis of the Talmud were reminded of both divine aspects. Significantly, of these two aspects, the quality of mercy was thought

---

1. Cohen, *Everyman's Talmud*, 16.

2. These names for God have different connotations, and some biblical authors prefer one to the other. But such distinctions are not at issue here.

to prevail. In fact, compassion was considered both the deciding cause of creation and the reason that God re-created human life after the great flood (Genesis 7–9).[3]

In Genesis 18, Abraham argues with God in order to dissuade God from destroying Sodom and Gomorrah. The rabbis interpreted that argument to mean that the world simply could not endure if God imposed such strict judgment.[4] Note that this view rejects the theology of retribution. Similarly, the rabbis interpreted the Torah's description of God as long-suffering to mean that God is fully as long-suffering with the wicked as with the righteous. They even considered God's patience and restraint with the wicked to be the greatest manifestation of God's power, so that the rabbis thought of God as much more the God of grace than the God of punishment. The Talmud says that even when angry, God remembers his mercy. The rabbis even imagined God praying to himself that his mercy would overcome his anger. Furthermore, Ezekiel 33:11 reads: "Say to them: As I live—declares the Lord God—it is not my desire that the wicked shall die, but that the wicked turn from his [evil] ways and live." The rabbis interpreted this passage to mean that when God can avert his wrath and display mercy, God rejoices. Hence, in the Talmud—and thus for most rabbis from several centuries BCE to the present—God is indeed Judge of the universe, but the judge who judges by grace.[5]

When the authors of the books of Jonah and Job protested against the then-predominant theology of retribution and defended the theology of grace, they could scarcely have imagined that their theology would, by the third century BCE, begin to gain a certain following among religious scholars and would, by the third or fourth century CE, become standard among Jews.

The authors of the four texts studied here would have had even greater difficulty imagining the Jesus movement. In the first century CE, a small group of dissenting Jews gathered around an itinerant preacher and healer called Jesus of Nazareth—a man

3. Ibid., 17.
4. Ibid., 17–18.
5. Ibid., 18–19.

clearly inspired by these same four texts. After Jesus' death, Jewish-Christian writers composed a significant body of literature about this Jesus, in which they artfully described how Jesus not only preached but—in his birth, life, death, and resurrection—embodied the theology of grace, as well as radical inclusivism and gender equality. The authors of the four liberal texts would have been amazed to learn that, through the Christian movement, the theology of grace not only spread rapidly across the Roman Empire but also preserved the important idea that grace is costly because it calls for significant changes in one's attitudes, values, and behavior. Consider, for example, what great changes the Ninevites undergo in the book of Jonah; they certainly do not take for granted the grace they have received.

Much later, in the Middle Ages, the church drastically undercut the theology of grace by claiming that Christians had to earn salvation through good works or even that salvation could simply be bought. But, contradicting those distortions, the Protestant Reformation powerfully re-asserted the theology of costly grace. Since the Reformation, however, the churches have repeatedly cheapened grace by failing to emphasize the dramatic personal transformations that God's grace aims to effect. U.S. synagogues and churches must take responsibility for this cheapening of grace because they have remained silent on important issues like war and peace, U.S. exceptionalism, armaments, torture, Bill Clinton's "humanitarian" wars, G.W. Bush's wars in Iraq and Afghanistan and his enhanced methods of interrogation and secret prisons, Obama's vigorous deportation of immigrants and widespread use of drones, the expenditure by the U.S. of roughly $1 trillion for nuclear weapons research, mass incarceration, police violence, persistent racism, growing xenophobia/nativism, voter suppression, to mention only a few of the important issues on which the synagogues and churches have maintained a cowardly silence, as if God's grace did not compel Christians and Jews to speak out on these issues.

As evidenced by the facts that Jesus' financial support comes from women (Luke 8:1–3): that Mary of Magdala sits at Jesus' feet

FINAL REFLECTIONS

like a real disciple (Luke 10:38); that, in the Gospels of Matthew, Mark, and Luke, it is women who come to his tomb to anoint his body; that in the Gospel of Mark women are closer to Jesus and more faithful to him than is anyone else, it is fair to say that Jesus dramatically embraces gender equality and rejects misogyny. Despite Jesus' example, however, the church rapidly became a patriarchal institution. Even today, in the Roman Catholic and Orthodox churches, the priesthood remains limited to men, and, as a result, women are marginalized. The mainline Protestant churches also tended historically to be patriarchal, and most did not begin ordaining women until the 1970s, although the Congregationalists began as early as the 1830s. The mainline Protestant churches have by now decided to welcome and affirm LGBTQ pastors and members, but in other U.S. churches, including Roman Catholic, Orthodox, and so-called evangelical churches, LGBTQ folks are at best tolerated and certainly not affirmed. Thus, these churches deny and reject the inclusivism and gender equality that are characteristic of the four texts studied here and—importantly—are also essential to the example set by Jesus.

Similarly, among Jews, women were excluded from the rabbinate until Hebrew Union College ordained a woman in 1972. Since then, both Reform and Conservative branches of Judaism have ordained women, including openly lesbian women. Recently, the number of female Orthodox religious scholars has grown remarkably, but Orthodox women have yet to be ordained.[6]

As for xenophobia among Jews, the policy of marrying only from within the Jewish community was practiced in the United States until the 1960s. Since then, however, intermarriage has become common and has aggravated the difficulty of maintaining Jewish identity.[7]

In conclusion, among both Jews and Christians, the long-term impact of the four texts studied in this book has been, at best, mixed. The theology of grace has been thoroughly disrespected and cheapened, primarily because both U.S. synagogues and

---

6. Telushkin, *Jewish Literacy*, 480–81.
7. Ibid., 492–96.

churches offer grace in the form of forgiveness of sins, without even suggesting that those who receive such grace should dramatically reform their thinking, their values, their behavior, and their opinions in relation to the important issues of their society. Such issues—if the synagogues and churches mention them at all—are simply left in God's hands, as if the believer had nothing directly to do with them.

In relation to xenophobia/nativism and misogyny, the record is also mixed. Overall, it is not clear how the four texts studied here overcame their rejection at the hands of the Jerusalem hardliners yet eventually came to exert some influence, however mixed, on both Jews and Christians.

The State of the Union

Since, in U.S. synagogues and churches, grace is effectively stripped of its costly character and given little more than lip service, it is not surprising that the theology of retribution predominates. As a result, it is not uncommon in the U.S. for the poor to be blamed for their own poverty. The poor are accused of being lazy and negligent or of lacking initiative, or of not respecting education, or of not knowing how to manage family life, or of preferring to live on welfare, etc. Ronald Reagan, speaking as President, famously referred to single mothers on welfare as "welfare queens." In other words, he claimed that single mothers both made a career out of dependence on welfare and abused that system at the same time. Reagan's remarks are a parade example of blaming the victim, and—importantly—the warrant for so doing is the theology of retribution. U.S. politicians routinely imitate Reagan by excusing their lack of legislative support for the homeless by claiming that some Americans simply prefer to live on the street. Again, the justification for such attitudes is the theology of retribution.

Neither is it uncommon in the U.S. for the wealthy to be looked up to as fonts of wisdom and exemplars of the American way of life. The explanation for such idol worship is not only ignorance but—importantly—the theology of retribution. For a

FINAL REFLECTIONS

surprising number of people in the U.S., material possessions are a sign of God's blessing, while poverty is somehow seen as a sign of God's punishment. For people who hold to the theology of retribution, a sufficiently wealthy person—despite egregious character flaws, a personal history of sharp practices, narcissism, misogyny, and utter disregard for others—can and even should be elected President.

As for xenophobia/nativism, the United States is a nation of immigrants, and the national myth is that we welcome immigrants and readily assimilate them into the proverbial melting pot. The reality, however, is quite different. The United States has a long and inglorious history of xenophobia and discrimination against immigrants, and against nonimmigrant minorities, too. Restrictive and punitive measures have targeted migrants because of their race and social class, and anti-immigrant sentiment has prevailed regardless of immigrants' demographic characteristics.[8] In one notorious case, the anti-immigration policies of the United States contributed to the humanitarian disaster that was the Holocaust, when the United States denied entry to European Jews fleeing Nazi persecution. Even the humane President Barack Obama ordered mass deportations of immigrants.

Xenophobia/nativism is, in fact, quite prevalent in the United States. Since the early 1980s there has been a resurgence of Klan violence. It is important to understand that the Klan is not only racist but also xenophobic, in that it perceives blacks as an economic threat. No longer does the Klan limit its activities to cross burnings and lynching; it now uses sophisticated language to influence others and to recruit on college campuses. The Klan even masquerades as public policy think-tanks in an attempt to influence public opinion and undo decades of progress in civil rights. The Klan also attempts to infiltrate public institutions, as was the case in Baltimore, where a well-known neo-Nazi lawyer was working for the city as defense attorney for the police.[9] But the churches remain silent on the question of the Klan.

8. Yakushko, "Xenophobia" 40–43.
9. The Southern Poverty Law Center, *Hate and Extremism in 2016*, 4–5.

The Struggle to Define God

Hate groups grew in numbers during Obama's tenure in office and now even use hate music to reach a young audience. The largest white supremacist forum, Stormfront, now has more than 300,000 registered members, an increase of 100 percent since the election of Obama in 2008. This hate forum is growing at the rate of 25,000 new members annually, at least in part because hate groups have become skilled in the use of social media.[10] But the churches remain silent on the question of hate groups and white supremacy.

Importantly, national events, such as the 2016 presidential election, are often catalysts for violent action. For example, the GOP primary campaign in 2015–2016 revealed shocking levels of bigotry and vitriol, with Donald Trump opening his campaign by claiming that Mexican immigrants were drug dealers and rapists. Note also that Trump prepared his run for the presidency by spreading the totally false "birther" conspiracy, which claimed that Obama is not an American citizen. Trump went on to announce his plan to deport eleven million people, build a border wall, and gut the fourteenth amendment, which guarantees citizenship to anyone born in the United States. Trump even claimed that a U.S. District judge was biased against him because the judge's parents were from Mexico.[11] But the churches and synagogues remained silent about these lies and threats.

In November 2015, Trump claimed—falsely—that Muslims in New Jersey had celebrated the attack on the World Trade Center on 9/11. Then, in the wake of the ISIS attacks in Paris, he called for a total ban on Muslim immigrants to the United States. When forty-nine people were killed at a gay nightclub in Orlando, Trump blamed the local Muslim community and hinted that President Obama was somehow complicit.[12] But the churches and synagogues remained silent.

These and similar statements earned Trump the support of white supremacist groups across America, including an

10. Ibid., 5.
11. SPLC Report, *SPLC Report puts Spotlight on Extremism in Presidential Campaign*, 5.
12. Ibid.

FINAL REFLECTIONS

endorsement from neo-Nazi David Duke. Another GOP primary contender, Ted Cruz, sought the support of the American Family Association, an anti-LGBT group known for spreading falsehoods about gays. In November 2015, GOP presidential contenders Cruz, Huckabee, and Jindal spoke at the National Religious Liberties Conference in Des Moines, Iowa, whose organizer, Kevin Swanson, has called for punishing homosexuals with death.[13] As the campaign continued, Trump's rallies grew more virulently nativist and violent,[14] and there were highly publicized examples of misogyny, too, involving an audio tape in which Trump boasted of sexually abusing women. Again, the sad fact is that U.S. synagogues and churches remained silent throughout the primary and general election campaigns, even when democracy and the very definition of God were under siege.

One of the most alarming examples of recent xenophobia/nativism in the United States is the vigilante anti-immigrant group called the Borderkeepers of Alabama, which is a heavily armed private army sent to patrol border towns. It claims that its mission is to secure our nation's borders against undocumented immigrants and drug smugglers. Borderkeepers is part of the nativist extremist movement that began around 2005 and that, by 2010, had grown to more than three-hundred groups. Since then, the movement's numbers have declined because state legislatures, especially in Alabama and Arizona, have passed harsh anti-immigrant laws.[15] But the churches and synagogues remain silent on the question of vigilantism and anti-immigrant laws.

In 2016, the Southern Poverty Law Center filed a complaint to stop the courts in Jefferson Parish, Louisiana, from discriminating against Latinos because of their national origin. The SPLC also participated in a federal lawsuit against the State of Georgia for violating federal law by denying driver's licenses to immigrants.[16]

13. Ibid.
14. Ibid.
15. The Southern Poverty Law Center, *Hate and Extremism in 2016*, 23–24
16. SPLC Report, *SPLC Report puts Spotlight on Extremism in Presidential Campaign*, 8.

The SPLC filed a lawsuit in 2016 against Kiawah Island Inn Golf Resort for illegally withholding $2.3 million in pay due to Jamaican guest workers who came to work at the resort. This was only the latest in a string of successful SPLC lawsuits against employers who defrauded and exploited guest workers.[17] But the churches and synagogues remain silent about such abuses.

These examples should be sufficient to demonstrate that xenophobia/nativism and misogyny are flourishing in the United States and that the churches and synagogues have not raised their voices in protest. Racism is also flourishing, but the churches and synagogues are silent on this problem, too. Unfortunately, racism is beyond the scope of this book since the four texts studied deal only with xenophobia/nativism and misogyny, but not with racism.

Importantly, the exit polls taken by PEW at the November 2016 Presidential elections indicate that—despite Jesus and the New Testament—voters who self-identify as Christians generally voted for Trump. Eighty-one percent of white, born again/evangelical Christians voted for Trump; sixty-one percent of Mormons voted for Trump; fifty-eight percent of Protestant/other Christian voted for Trump; fifty-two percent of Catholics voted for Trump; sixty percent of white Catholics voted for Trump. On the other hand, a large majority of Hispanic Catholics, Black Christians, Jews, people of other faiths, and the religiously unaffiliated voted for Hillary Clinton.[18] Thus, any claim that predominantly white U.S. churches have taught their members to defend Christian values or overcome xenophobia/nativism and misogyny seems dubious. White Christians voted overwhelmingly for the candidate who proudly and unapologetically ran on a platform of xenophobia/nativism and misogyny and who constantly pandered to the American idolatry of wealth. Of course, Clinton had her shortcomings, too, but by no stretch of the imagination was she a sociopathic, xenophobic misogynist. In fact, she had a very respectable record of public service. Overall, the election of Trump erases any optimism one might have had about U.S. Christians' learning to follow Jesus.

17. Ibid., 1.
18. *The Religious Vote*, 9.

Final reflections

Some of those self-identified Christians who voted for Trump might say that they did so despite his checkered past, despite his narcissism, despite his authoritarianism, despite his worship of wealth and power, despite his unsavory associations, despite his blatant xenophobia/nativism, despite his crude misogyny, despite his demagoguery, etc. It is certainly possible that some Trump voters may have liked part of Trump or part of his message but disliked the rest. Yet the inconvenient and rather obvious truth is that a vote for Trump—whatever the reason—affirmed and endorsed the whole Trump, with all his undemocratic, un-Christian, and sociopathic baggage. Given the legal restraints on U.S. churches and on other charitable institutions regarding political speech, no one expected the churches to speak out for or against Trump during the campaign, but it is certainly reasonable to expect that, long before the elections, churches would have given their members sufficient instruction to enable them to identify and reject any such candidate. It also is reasonable to expect that, even during the campaign, the churches would speak out against blatantly un-Christian speech and action, as well as against obvious dangers to our democratic system. But again the churches were silent.

Overall, the fact that Trump owes his election to white, allegedly Christian voters speaks to the gross unfaithfulness of many U.S. churches, which have failed to tell people that the grace they receive calls for them to leave their old life behind—with all its prejudices and resentments—and to become new beings in Christ. It goes without saying that a new being in Christ, though not necessarily voting for Clinton, would not vote for Donald J. Trump under any circumstances.

Conclusions

The question, then, is what—if anything—can be done about the decidedly un-Christ-like attitude and behavior of those many millions of self-identified Christians who, in their behavior at political rallies and in their voting, opted for the opposite of everything Jesus stood for? Should one expect that they will repent?

The Struggle to Define God

The Hebrew Bible has only a few examples of bad actors who, on their own initiative, repent and change their ways. One thinks especially of Judah, who, in Genesis 37:26–27, callously proposes to his brothers that, because they have nothing to gain by killing their brother Joseph, they should instead sell him to the Ishmaelites. But later, in Genesis 44:33–34, when Jacob's youngest son, Benjamin, is in danger of being held hostage in Egypt, Judah shows that he is a changed man, by offering to stay in Egypt as a slave so that Benjamin can return to his father.[19]

In 2 Samuel 12, David repents after having committed adultery with Bathsheba and having arranged for her husband, Uriah, to be killed in battle. But this repentance doesn't really count as spontaneous because the prophet Nathan shames David into it.

In fact, the biblical model for repentance (*teshuvah*) is not the spontaneous type. It is rather the type engineered by God. If human beings readily turned to God on their own initiative, it would not have been necessary for God to destroy humankind in the great flood or to work so hard to keep Israel faithful. What is true of repentance in the Hebrew Bible is also true for any significant change in human beings. That is, when people change, it is because God changed them. The Hebrew Bible is a kind of history of such changes. God changes the homebody Abram (later Abraham) into an adventurer willing to wander with God to places unknown. By means of a near-death experience at the ford of the river Jabbok, God changes Jacob from swindler to father of a great nation. When the Israelites are slaves in Egypt, they don't free themselves; God frees them. Those who experience the Babylonian exile don't decide on their own to become monotheists; God makes them into monotheists. Throughout the Hebrew Bible, God transforms people and re-creates them as they ought to be. That same metaphor of destruction/re-creation runs all the way through the New Testament, too. No one saves himself from sin; God does it. No one on his own initiative abandons his old life and follows Christ; God makes it happen.

---

19. In fact, even Judah's change does not proceed from his own initiative, because it comes as the result of his being embarrassed by Tamar (Genesis 38).

FINAL REFLECTIONS

Thus, the final suggestion of this book is not that one should try to reason with Donald Trump and his supporters; they have already demonstrated an astounding capacity for denying the evidence. It would make more sense to ask God to transform such people into what they ought to be.

Only God can effect such profound changes, but, apart from rare cases of direct divine intervention, God usually uses human individuals or communities to change attitudes, values, and behavior. Consider, for example, how many people changed because of the example set by Martin Luther King Jr.

The fact that God works through human individuals and communities leads to the question of the church's role in the world. Through its teaching, preaching, and public example, the church is supposed to be the institutional equivalent of Dr. King—God's instrument for changing attitudes, values, and behavior, and making these more Christ-like. But the church can do this only if it preaches the Gospel boldly and in undiluted form—that is, with powerful emphasis on costly grace, loving inclusivism, and gender equality.

Thus, the fact that all positive change has its origins in God certainly does not mean that we are left with nothing to do. God seeks partners, so that whatever transformations God performs on us are designed to make us into more active and more Christ-like partners with God. And we humans, within the limits of our ability, can certainly cooperate with God and contribute in incremental ways. In any case, being transformed by God, whether dramatically or incrementally, means that we develop into partners with God, and such growth includes our becoming—not merely passive recipients of grace—but active and more effective leaders. (Since the goal of the transformations that God performs is the development of leaders, it is appropriate to say something about leadership. See below: Addendum on Leadership).

The mission of both the synagogue and the church is to help and encourage people to go through a process of adaptive change—that is, change in their attitudes, values, and behavior. Once people have gone through these changes, their mission is to promote adaptive changes in others, too, until the whole society

The Struggle to Define God

has changed for the better. Both Jews and Christians are called to build incrementally on the transformation that God has performed on them and to engage in critical thinking, innovation, and action to promote adaptive change. Such is the covenantal responsibility of both the synagogue and the church.

Historically, Judaism has placed great emphasis on ethical and effective partnership with God, as evidenced, for example, by the fact that U.S. Jews have maintained a profound distrust of demagogic leaders and have instead understood leadership to be humble service.[20] The model for such attitudes and behavior is Moses, who is remembered as the humblest man on earth.[21] For all these reasons and perhaps for others, too, Jews voted overwhelmingly against Donald Trump. Thus, it seems fair to say that U.S synagogues are doing at least something right. Jesus also understood leadership to be humble service: "If anyone would be first, he must be last of all and servant of all" (Mark 9:35). Sadly, many white, so-called Christians in the U.S. have not understood or accepted this biblical understanding of service, as evidenced by the fact that they voted for a blatantly un-Christian, sociopathic demagogue widely regarded as one of the least humble men on earth.

The four texts studied in this book—the story of Rahab and the books of Job, Jonah, and Ruth—are brilliant, well-intentioned attempts to encourage people to grow and change by overcoming their fears, resentments, and prejudices, so that they can become gracious, loving, and inclusive like God and thus be partners with God. Following this same pattern, the New Testament makes clear that if one is to follow Jesus, one must, in humble repentance, undergo such adaptive changes—not once in a lifetime but every day. This study indicates, however, that many U.S. churches—especially the so-called evangelical churches—have simply failed to promote such changes in their members and, instead, have allowed or even encouraged people to define God in ways that serve to justify their own resentments, prejudices, or personal interests. In short, these churches have permitted their people to think wrongly about God,

---

20. Ibid., 186–87 and 207.
21. Numbers 12:3.

and if people are thinking wrongly about God, then they are not actually thinking about God at all. Clearly, these churches have broken their covenant with God.

It is time, then, for these churches to confess their unfaithfulness, ask God to re-make them into what they ought to be, and then get busy doing what God expects of them.

Addendum on Leadership

When times are hard, and people feel threatened, they yearn for technical solutions and tend to select authoritative leaders to whom they can defer.[22] Donald Trump correctly sensed that tendency and ran as an authority figure, even claiming that he would fix the country's problems all by himself. In times of stress, this kind of demagoguery can have great popular appeal. Unfortunately, however, authoritative leadership is seldom appropriate. Why isn't it?

Authoritative leadership most often fails because it misdiagnoses the problems.[23] Because the authoritative leader possesses technical expertise and is accustomed to being in command, he tends to see most issues as technical or as problems that he can solve by issuing directives. For example, Trump's alleged expertise is deal-making, and so he naturally thinks that the country's problem is that we have made bad deals, which he can fix by making better deals. Moreover, he assumes that all the social and political systems and norms are already in place, so that he can simply apply his expertise, issue his commands, and solve our problems. As one can readily recognize, authoritative leadership, by its very nature, generates dependency,[24] which is certainly not what God desires; God wants active partners and leaders.

The reality is that our problems are not technical; they are mostly adaptive and require adaptive leadership—that is, leadership that encourages us to learn, grow, and change our attitudes,

---

22. Sacks, *Lessons in Leadership*, xv.
23. Ibid.
24. Ibid., xvi.

values, and behavior. Adaptive problems also require us to develop social and political systems and norms that do not yet exist. Problems like poverty, terrorism, climate change, gender equality, racism, or immigration do not have technical solutions; they require a change in attitude and behavior among large numbers of people and can be solved only if people work together. Because the changes required are far-reaching and involve attitudes, values, and behavior, solutions must come from the bottom up. Authoritative leadership is top-down and will not work; it is simply not possible to command such changes. [25] The adaptive leadership we need must inspire critical thinking, innovation, passion, and action at the local level—that is, adaptive leadership should generate capacity to resolve problems at the grass-roots level.

Importantly, leadership and authority are distinctly different, and that distinction becomes crucial if the problems at hand are adaptive. One has authority by holding an office or by occupying a certain position in the company, family or hierarchy. But people with authority do not necessarily promote the change that adaptive problems call for—that is, they do not necessarily lead. In the exodus story, for example, the Pharaoh, though quite authoritative, does everything he can to prevent change. On the other hand, one can lead even if one has no authority.[26] The parade example of an unauthoritative but influential leader is Moses, who initially is clumsy but gradually learns how to lead. Pharaoh has all the authority and power, but Moses gains more and more leadership and influence. And Moses eventually achieves the desired change. Furthermore, from the exodus onward, Moses makes many mistakes but grows steadily in his leadership skills. His example shows that one is not born with leadership ability; insteadone develops it through trial and error.

Significantly, the covenant that both the churches and the synagogues have with God calls for them to develop their members into the influential adaptive leaders that God wants as partners.

---

25. Donald Trump may have excellent technical abilities, but the task at hand calls for entirely different skills.

26. Sacks, *Lessons in Leadership*, xxii–iv.

Bibliography

Butterfield, Robert. *Making Sense of the Hebrew Bible*. Eugene: Wipf and Stock, 2016.

Cohen, Abraham. *Everyman's Talmud*. New York: Schocken, 1949.

Jewish Publication Society. *JPS Hebrew-English Tanakh: The Traditional Hebrew Text and the New JPS Translation*. Philadelphia: Jewish Publication Society, 1999.

Lenz, Ryan and Mark Potok. *Hate and Extremism in 2016*. Montgomery, AL: Southern Poverty Law Center.

———. *SPLC Report—Fall 2016*. Montgomery, AL: Southern Poverty Law Center.

Sacks, Jonathan. *Lessons in Leadership: A Weekly Reading of the Jewish Bible*. Jerusalem: Maggid, 2015.

Schama, Simon. *A História dos Judeus: Encontrar as palavras, 1000 AC—1492 DC*. Lisbon: Círculo de Leitores e Temas e Debates, 2013.

Telushkin, Joseph. *Jewish Literacy*. New York: HarperCollins, 2008.

"The Religious Vote." *The Christian Century*, December 6, 2016.

Yakushko, Oksana. "Xenophobia: Understanding the Roots and Consequences of Negative Attitudes toward Immigrants." In *Educational Psychology Papers and Publications*. Paper 90. http://digital.commons.unl.edu/psychpapers/90, 2009.

www.ingramcontent.com/pod-product-compliance
Lightning Source LLC
Chambersburg PA
CBHW070517090426
42735CB00012B/2814